NORTH CAROLINA
IN THE

1940s

NORTH CAROLINA

IN THE

1940s

THE **DECADE** OF **TRANSFORMATION**

PHILIP GERARD

BLAIR

Blair is an imprint of Carolina Wren Press.

CWP

The mission of Blair/Carolina Wren Press is to seek out, nurture, and promote literary work by new and underrepresented writers.

We gratefully acknowledge the ongoing support of general operations by the Durham Arts Council's United Arts Fund and the North Carolina Arts Council.

Designed by Jason Chenier and Miranda Young

ISBN: 978-1-949467-82-6
Library of Congress Control Number: 2022934104

ALSO BY PHILIP GERARD

The Art of Creative Research

Cape Fear Rising

Down the Wild Cape Fear:
A River Journey Through the Heart of North Carolina

The Dark of the Island

Hatteras Light

The Last Battleground:
The Civil War Comes to North Carolina

The Patron Saint of Dreams

Things We Do When No One Is Watching

CONTENTS

CONTENTS

THE **DECADE** OF **TRANSFORMATION**

The 1940s is the decade when Depression turns into prosperity, when disillusionment gives way to optimism, when want yields to plenty—and when domestic peace is shattered by world war. It is the heyday of Hollywood movie stars like Ingrid Bergman, Humphrey Bogart, Lauren Bacall, Katharine Hepburn, and Clark Gable. A farmer's daughter from a North Carolina country crossroads called Grabtown—Ava Gardner—personifies the big-screen mythos of dangerous, seductive beauty as Kitty Collins in the film version of Ernest Hemingway's story "The Killers." The movies turn glamour into a national obsession.

But as the decade opens, North Carolina remains largely a place of farms and small towns, its people aware of the faraway new war in Europe and slowly emerging from hard times as if waking from a bad fever dream. Many farmers still plow behind mules. Milk and beer are delivered by horse-drawn wagons. When night falls across the coastal plain between towns, across the great swath of Piedmont farmland, over the mountains of the western counties, the darkness erases the land. An airmail pilot flying the route from Richmond to Raleigh and on to Charlotte would see a black map below beyond the loom of the cities.

In 1940, fewer than one in four farms is powered by electricity—leaving more than two hundred thousand others in the dark. Little more than a decade later, nearly all farmsteads are electrified. Indoor plumbing, too, comes to rural communities. Men and women are working again and earning real wages.

But progress does not come equally to all. Waiting rooms and restrooms are designated "white" and "colored." Blacks often are paid less than whites for the same labor. Even Black men who enlisted in the Civilian Conservation Corps, where they earn the same thirty dollars per month as their white counterparts, are housed in segregated camps.

Tobacco is king—the greatest wealth generator in the state. The fall tobacco auction is the most important event of the season, and the market at Wilson is the largest in the world. Cigarettes—ubiquitous both on the screen and in the audience of local movie houses—sell for twelve cents a pack.

For those with cash money, there are bargains to be had. Ladies' wool winter coats can be purchased at the Collins Department Store in Charlotte or Whiteville for $2.75 each, boys' all-wool suits for just $1.19. At the Pender Quality Food Stores, spinach goes for ten cents a pound, Land O'Lakes American cheese for twenty-one cents a pound, and skinless franks for nineteen cents a pound. An eighteen-ounce loaf of bread costs just eight cents.

An Apex automatic washing machine can be bought for less than fifty dollars, a bedroom suite for less than sixty dollars. An Elgin bicycle is available from Sears Roebuck for $22.88.

Automobiles are sleek and fast—like the 1940 Ford Deluxe V-8 coupe favored by moonshiners—and promise not only speed but also status. Whiteville Motors sells the 1940 Dodge Luxury Liner coupe for $725. Its competitor, Braxton Auto Service, offers an Oldsmobile sedan ("Feels, Measures Bigger!") for $853. The gasoline they guzzle costs just eighteen cents per gallon.

Across the state, traveling big bands play hotel ballrooms in the cities and small local auditoriums in the heartland in full throat, and the radio reaches into newly electrified farmsteads, an invisible net of voices and music: speeches, comedies, variety shows, swing bands, and the border music of high lonesome tenors and twangy guitars and fiddles.

One of those radio stations is WBT in Charlotte—the first fully licensed commercial radio station south of Washington, D.C. In 1949, WBT launches a companion television station, marking the end of the Golden Age of radio.

Kay Kyser's big band starts as a student group at the University of North Carolina. Out of Rocky Mount comes jazz pianist Thelonious Monk and from Hamlet saxophonist John Coltrane—just two of the many jazz legends in the making. Down at Freeman's Beach just north of Carolina Beach, Seabreeze resort is in full swing—three hotels, ten restaurants, a bingo parlor, a boat pier, dozens of rental cottages, and an amusement park with a Ferris wheel—catering to African Americans. At night Seabreeze resounds with brassy music from the likes of Count Basie and Duke Ellington.

In 1942, a fatherless kid named Earl Scruggs graduates Boiling Springs High School and sets out to become a musician—playing his banjo with a new three-finger roll method on the radio in Spartanburg, South Carolina. One of his fans turns out to be Bill Monroe, who invites Scruggs to join him with the Blue Grass Boys on the Grand Ole Opry.

Big band swing, hot jazz, mountain border music, low country blues, and bluegrass are the soundtrack of this decade of restless movement, striving, and optimism.

All across North Carolina, it is a decade of economic and social transformation: nearly a third of a million farms—where 40 percent of the population lives—reap bumper crops of cotton, soybeans, peanuts, corn, hogs, and tobacco. The dairy industry doubles its output. On the Roanoke River, the Tillery Farms Project—a program of President Franklin D. Roosevelt's New Deal—lifts hundreds of white and Black families out of tenant farming poverty and helps them become owners of their own farms.

Every small town fields a newspaper and most cities more than one, cheap and available through delivery or mail. A reader can subscribe to both the Wilmington weekday *Morning Star* and Sunday *News*, for example, for just thirty cents a week—and keep up with local and national affairs and chuckle over the antics of Alley Oop, Wash Tubbs, the Gumps, Little Orphan Annie, and the crew of Gasoline Alley. War looms over the country, and the daily headlines announce Russian advances in Finland, Nazi U-Boats hunting in the Atlantic, and rising tensions between the Roosevelt administration and the Japanese government. The public mood remains optimistic, even ebullient—as the impending war brings jobs, investment, and prosperity to many communities—until the stunning attack on Pearl Harbor and the declaration of war bring anxiety, separation, uncertainty, and loss.

An old field artillery training ground, Camp Bragg, previously slated for decommissioning, instead opens its gates to an influx of one hundred thousand soldiers—including all five airborne divisions in the U.S. Army. Nearby Fayetteville—population seventeen thousand—is overrun with troops preparing to wage a new kind of mechanized warfare.

On November 4, 1941, the Associated Press (AP) reports, "The greatest concentration of anti-tank forces the Army has ever assembled in one maneuver area moved across the Carolinas today waiting for the armored division's thrust against the First Army." The mock battle culminates on a ridge south of Charlotte in a melee of 350 tanks and other vehicles.

On the same day as the AP report, the *Wilmington Star* commemorates the passing of Aunt Esther Gore, a formerly enslaved person, at the county home: "Up until recently the centenarian had been unusually active and clear of mind, despite her advanced age." She was 107 years old. Thus the living memory of the Civil War fades into the reality of world war.

A fourteen-mile-long swath of coastal land outside Jacksonville is chosen to host a new Marine Corps base—Camp Lejeune—where as many as forty-two thousand marines train in amphibious combat in the overgrown coastal thickets and on the Onslow Bay beaches. By executive order of President Roosevelt, the marines enlist the first of twenty thousand African Americans to train in a segregated base called Montford Point.

By 1942, North Carolina—with more than one hundred military installations—is home to more soldiers, sailors, Coast Guardsmen, and marines than any other state in the Union. More than 10 percent of the state's population—362,500 men and women—serve in the armed forces, and more than 9,000 of them never return home.

Just south of Wilmington, a new fleet of cargo ships sprouts almost overnight on the east bank of the Cape Fear River—the Liberty Ships. They slide down the slipways at the rate of one per week for more than four years—designed to carry food, ammunition, tanks, bombers, fighter planes, artillery, and gasoline to the war.

To power the growing defense industry, the Tennessee Valley Authority begins construction of the massive Fontana Dam on the Little Tennessee River in 1942, finishing the project in just three years—the workers put in seven-day weeks.

The 480-foot-high dam—the highest in the Tennessee Valley

chain and the tallest east of the Rockies—is built of three million cubic yards of concrete and generates 202.5 megawatts of electricity per day. It is such a sensation that it draws hundreds of visitors—one of them existentialist philosopher and writer Jean-Paul Sartre, who visits on a press junket in 1944.

To house the five thousand workers in such a remote location (distant even from Asheville and an hour from Robbinsville), the engineers construct an entire new town of prefabricated houses and dormitories: Fontana. After the dam is completed, all the temporary workers leave the town, and it remains virtually deserted until reopened as a private resort in 1946.

Natural disasters, fights for workers' rights, and disease take their toll on North Carolina throughout the decade.

In August 1940, five days of torrential rain in the mountain counties causes a great flood and two thousand massive landslides on mountainsides clear-cut by the great timber companies. Entire communities at Grandfather Mountain, Deep Gap, and Mortimer are swept away. The railroad to Boone is washed out, never to run again. NC Highway 411 to Wilkesboro is cut. The French Broad carries away the bridge at Marshall, and the Tuckasegee River rampages. That same month, twenty-one inches of rainfall turn downtown Boone into a muddy lake. At least sixteen people are killed.

Hundreds of miles to the east, the coast is slammed by the Great Atlantic Hurricane of 1944, which damages or destroys almost eight hundred homes. On Hatteras Island, a federal barrier dunes project gets underway to protect against future storm surge, and at long last, the state department of transportation begins paving sandy Highway 12.

Textile factory production ebbs and flows with a constant tension between workers and owners—then revs up to meet the demands of the new war for uniforms, tents, tarpaulins. Tobacco factories cope with their own labor unrest—culminating in a strike by ten thousand workers at the R. J. Reynolds plant in Winston-Salem. The tension between labor and owners plays out at textile and tobacco mills across the state as part of "Operation Dixie," an attempt to champion workers and civil rights— but ultimately the owners win.

In the far west, the Eastern Band of Cherokee fight against termination of the protected status of their lands—and for tribal identity. The Cherokee Historical Association actively promotes the Eastern Cherokee legacy. Alert to the postwar tourist crowds—arriving in the family automobile—the Eastern Cherokee stage performances to celebrate their culture and build a hotel and visitor center at the entrance to Great Smoky Mountains National Park. Cherokee war veterans now insist on the right to vote—previously denied them.

In Chapel Hill and Raleigh and other cities, returning veterans mob college campuses to take advantage of the G. I. Bill of Rights. New state colleges open in Wilmington and Charlotte. Black Mountain College—offering an alternative curriculum that integrates academics, the arts, and practical skills—is going strong. Visiting luminaries include Buckminster Fuller and Albert Einstein. Elsewhere in North Carolina, poet Randall Jarrell and novelist Robert Ruark are at work on promising literary careers—Ruark already a syndicated household name.

Polio—the same scourge that attacked President Roosevelt in his prime—strikes North Carolina in two waves: in 1944 the epidemic engulfs Hickory and, four years later, Greensboro. On both occasions, emergency hospitals are established to treat white and Black patients together—with an integrated medical staff. In 1948, the peak of the polio threat, 2,516 children are struck with the disease and 43 die—far fewer than the expected number. Their success is remembered as the "Miracle of Hickory." The twin ordeals lead North Carolina to become the first state to require that schoolchildren be vaccinated with Jonas Salk's new vaccine.

Presiding over nearly the entire decade from the governor's mansion in Raleigh is Joseph Melville Broughton. A rock-solid public servant with a sober demeanor, he beats six Democratic primary opponents in 1940 and wins by the largest majority in a gubernatorial election up to that time.

As governor, he raises teachers' salaries, institutes a retirement plan for state employees, adds a twelfth grade to high school, and extends the school calendar to nine months, as well as leading other progressive achievements in health care and the corrections department.

His reliable leadership carries the state across the threshold of a new era of electrified farms; burgeoning cities; military preparedness; educational progress; the first tentative, significant stirrings of racial equality since Reconstruction; and an economy that is paying off for North Carolinians in all walks of life.

Crews prepare the SS *Zebulon B. Vance* for its launch from the North Carolina shipbuilding company, which stood at the site of the current Port of Wilmington.

CHAPTER

THE
LIBERTY ARMADA

As the decade turns from the calamitous 1930s—with its stock market crash and bank failures, its Dust Bowl and Depression, its unemployment and hunger—to the restless 1940s, war appears more and more inevitable. The *Whiteville News Reporter* offers its readers "New Year's Greetings—Peace on Earth 1940" but days later announces, "National Defense Expansion Urged by the President."

In local newspapers across the state, sandwiched between ads for feed and appliances and new cars, headlines bring the war ever closer. The *New York Times* reports on November 1, 1941, "Reuben James Hit—First American Warship Lost in War Torpedoed West of Iceland." Seventy-seven officers and men of the destroyer USS *Reuben James* remain missing, feared dead. The story resonates with locals: the skipper, Lieut. Cmdr. Heywood L. "Tex" Edwards, married a Wilmington girl, Almeda Stewart, just six years prior. The same month, the tanker *Salinas* is reported sunk by a U-boat.[1]

The United States of America, with peaceful neighbors to the north and south, is essentially a continental island. To wage war against either the Germans or the Japanese means crossing an ocean—Atlantic or Pacific—and that requires ships. From colonial times through the Civil War and during the Great War, the Cape Fear River has been the site of shipyards, but no new ship has been built here since 1918. Now the North Carolina Shipbuilding Company—a subsidiary of the Newport News Shipbuilding and Dry Dock Company—sets up on the east bank of the Cape Fear. Wilmington has won its first wartime battle—against rival Morehead City, which has been actively lobbying to become the shipyard site.

Newport News Shipbuilding is renowned for the craftsmanship and teamwork of its shipwrights, and the company has never endured a strike in half a century of operation. In its apprentice program, selected high school graduates receive four to five years of paid production experience and training.

But the company is also anti-union, and almost from the start of operations, the Wilmington site is locked into an ongoing dispute with the Congress of Industrial Organizations (CIO). The CIO contends that workers who join unions are often reassigned to dangerous or menial jobs and are the first to be terminated. The hearings of the National Labor Relations Board drag on until the war is long over, and the complaint is at last settled with a lump sum payment of back wages to aggrieved workers.

The president of Newport News Shipbuilding is Homer Lenoir Ferguson—a Waynesville, North Carolina, native, son of a Confederate veteran. His strict Scotch-Irish upbringing instilled in him a fierce work ethic and an abiding respect for those who worked with their hands—including Blacks. He routinely hires Black workers for skilled positions such as machinist, riveter, engineer, or welder.

He was elevated to lead the company after his predecessor,

A. L. Hopkins, went down on the torpedoed *Lusitania* in the Great War. Ferguson is sixty-eight years old, a U.S. Naval Academy graduate who studied naval architecture in Glasgow, Scotland—the nation that produced the revolutionary and fast blockade runners for the Confederates during the Civil War. Ferguson is handsome and fit, a can-do leader who inspires confidence in his superiors and loyalty in his workers and is always alert to innovation—though at times frustrated when others claim credit for his work, as too often happened in the navy. His code: "Always give credit where credit is due, to those working over you, with you, or under you."[2] After overseeing the construction of five battleships and a cruiser for the navy, he had enough and joined the private shipbuilder.

The plan for the Cape Fear shipyard is straightforward and efficient: construct thirty-seven new cargo ships, at a cost of $42 million, to a uniform design adopted from the British and used by all American shipyards—which can be modified for tankers and fitted with anti-aircraft guns—and carry supplies to England through the Lend-Lease Act of 1941. Rather than using the traditional expensive and time-consuming method of riveting steel plates, workers will build the ships in modules and weld the pieces together—a risky technique that has not been tried much in oceangoing ships. No one really expects the ships to hold up for more than a few years, but speed and efficiency are worth the risk.[3]

Roger Williams, another Annapolis alum, is named president of the new North Carolina Shipbuilding Company. In 1917, Ferguson championed the building of Hilton Village to house the influx of workers required to meet war demand at Newport News—and his innovation is replicated in a hundred more pioneering government housing projects, including—now—at Wilmington.

The company harnesses federal subsidies to create three

housing projects for some nine hundred workers. Greenfield Terrace, of permanent construction, houses 300 white families with rents starting at $27.50 per month. Lake Village, of "demountable" temporary fabrication, houses another 475 white families. And the 126 Black families find homes in Hillcrest Extension, a permanent community with rents of $18–$22.

The two white communities are located near Greenfield Lake, just north of the shipyard and an easy commute away. Housing for Black workers is located at Dawson at 14th and 15th Streets— several miles away. Buses serve all three communities—some of the fleet of 140 trucks and buses ferrying workers back and forth between Wilmington and the beach towns—and also from places as far away as Whiteville, Fairmont, Lumberton, and St. Paul's. When the whistle blows signaling end of shift, workers sprint from the gates for more than a block to gain a seat on the homebound bus—or else be forced to stand as "strap-hangers."

Work gangs are integrated—with white and Black men working alongside one another in a range of skilled and unskilled jobs—but dining, restroom, and locker facilities are strictly segregated. White workers read the *Shipyard Bulletin*; their Black counterparts enjoy the *Colored Shipbuilder*.

Discrimination by Maritime Commission contractors is prohibited by Roosevelt's own executive order, but practice does not always follow the law. During periodic racial tensions, Blacks and whites exit the yard through separate gates.

In a matter of months, the shipyard takes shape on 56.9 riverside acres—including its own bus terminal, cafeteria, police and fire departments, even a hospital. Four hundred Newport News employees are transferred down from Virginia, but more than five hundred men and women are recruited locally: plumbers, carpenters, and electricians, along with unskilled trainees who will have to learn on the job.[4]

At first, women are relegated to less strenuous jobs, but

quickly they prove their abilities and take on heavier jobs such as plumbing and welding. They dress in slacks and blouses and find work shoes where they can—a difficult task, since steel-toed boots are manufactured only in men's sizes. Many wear Boy Scout shoes or regular open-toed footwear, and broken toes are a constant hazard. The yard is swarming with workers twenty-four hours a day in three shifts, but women are allowed to work only the first two—never the graveyard shift, and never below decks of a vessel, to avoid compromising situations. The company provides on-site daycare for their young children, though young women without children are most valued as workers.

Building Liberty Ships was dangerous and deadly. Some 115,000 workers were injured and 15 died during the five years the North Carolina shipbuilding company was in operation.

Shipbuilding is hazardous work: laborers shift giant turbines and monstrous steel side panels with locomotive and "whirley" cranes that can rotate 360 degrees, handle gas-powered welding torches and power saws, and clamber into tight spaces and onto high catwalks laden with heavy tools. Much of the work is done outdoors in all weather. Despite large signs at the gates admonishing WORK SAFELY, Wilmington suffers an accident rate nearly twice the average for American shipyards: 115,000 injuries, an additional 81 accidents that result in maiming or permanent disability, and 15 deaths on the job.[5]

The pace of the seven-day workweek is relentless. Robert S. Pollock, a young apprentice who works his way up to installing main propulsion engines as a steam engineer, records: "On one occasion I worked 23 hours—on May 31, 1943, when the NC shipyard set a record by commissioning 11 ships from 9 shipways that month."[6]

At night the yard is illuminated by nearly two thousand floodlights, with an unintended, dangerous consequence: captains of vessels passing off Cape Fear complain that on cloudy nights with no moon, they are silhouetted against the bright loom of the yard, making them perfect targets for U-boats. On the night of March 12, 1942, the tanker *John D. Gill*, bound for Philadelphia, is torpedoed and sunk off the mouth of the river. Future sea trials for newly commissioned vessels are conducted entirely inside the river.

The yard keeps growing, eventually housing a shop for a new high-speed turbine gear so secret that the shop is left off maps of the site. Within two years, the shipyard employs twenty-five thousand people and dispenses a payroll of $50 million a year—transforming Wilmington into a lively boomtown as young workers with money to spend mingle with soldiers, sailors, and marines at the growing collection of USOs, bars, and nightclubs after shift.

The USO on Second and Orange, open twenty-four hours

a day, seven days a week, becomes one such social hub. Junior Hostesses and Liberty Belles dance with servicemen, mend their uniforms, and serve them refreshments.

Before it launches a single vessel, the shipyard is clouded by controversy. The first of the designated "Liberty Ships," scheduled to come off the ways in December, will be named *Francis Marion*—honoring the Revolutionary War guerrilla leader from South Carolina. Others are to be named for Nathanael Greene and Daniel Morgan—Revolutionary War generals from Rhode Island and New Jersey, respectively—and four more South

On July 30, 1943, the SS *James I. McKay* was christened in Wilmington by Mary West Cromartie, a descendant of the ship's namesake, a North Carolina congressman from the 1800s.

Carolinians: John C. Calhoun, Charles C. Pinckney, William Moultrie, and Edward Rutledge.

The naming choices strike a blow to local pride. The *Star* reports without byline that the Wilmington Chamber of Commerce is protesting to Admiral Emory S. Land, chair of the United States Maritime Commission: "Thus, it would appear that, to date, South Carolina has gained more recognition than any other state in the number of vessels constructed here."

Just weeks before the launch, the commission accedes to the protest: the new vessel instead will be christened *Zebulon B. Vance*—after the lionized Civil War governor of North Carolina. The ship will stretch 441 feet, 6 inches in length with a beam of 56 feet, displacing 14,100 tons and drafting 27 feet, 8 inches. Powered by a single steam turbine generating 2,500 horsepower for a cruising speed of up to 11 knots, the *Vance* will be manned by 44 officers and crew and carry more than 9,000 tons of cargo: 440 tanks, 2,840 Jeeps, or 230 million rounds of small arms ammunition. The price tag is steep: $1,610,000.

"It will become a cog in the great wheel of defense," reports the *Star*. "It will be used to move Martin bombers to Europe, to move ore to steel mills, to move food to Russia and to move thousands of other items that make up the commerce of this nation and its defense effort. The *Vance* and hundreds of its sister ships being built at yards on every coast of this nation will make up the greatest commercial armada in history."[7]

The Greater Wilmington Chamber of Commerce sponsors a laudatory congratulations under the headline "There She Goes": "Bon Voyage to you, oh good ship ZEBULON B. VANCE! Wilmington-made you have aboard a full cargo of Wilmington Pride. May good fortune always attend you as you carry the Stars and Stripes of a Free Country through the troubled waters of the world."[8]

The *Vance* will be loaded immediately after being fitted

out—and will carry Wilmington port's first lend-lease cargo.

The launching is set for noon on December 6. Newport News Company president Ferguson presides, opening the short ceremony with brief remarks, followed by Capt. Edmund Macauley of the U.S. Maritime Commission. Gov. Joseph Melville Broughton also addresses the crowd—the winner of the largest gubernatorial vote in the state's history, honoring the legacy of another wartime governor who won by a landslide. His wife, Alice Wilson Broughton, christens the ship with the traditional bottle of champagne.

Two of Gov. Vance's descendants attend as guests on the dais: Harriet Espay Vance Cobb, widow of Vance's grandson from Mobile, Alabama; and John C. Vance, a member of the Buncombe County Board of Commissioners.

Admission to the event requires a card issued by the North Carolina Shipbuilding Company. It has given its workers a holiday and urged them to bring their families to witness the inaugural launch, and an additional fifteen thousand spectators are ushered into a reserved viewing area.[9]

The *Vance* is the first of 243 ships to be built at Wilmington, of both Liberty and the faster Victory design—twenty-seven of which will be sunk by the enemy.[10]

But the *Vance* is lucky: on the dreaded Murmansk run, it survives a torpedo attack and floating mines, then serves in the transport fleet for the invasion of North Africa, and later does duty as a hospital ship renamed USS *John J. Meany*. Its final duty in the war is to transport war brides home from Europe.

But all that lies in the turbulent future.

As spectators mob the riverbanks, the *Vance*—rigging festooned stem to stern with nautical flags—slides stern-first down the ways and plunges into the river, sending a tannin-brown wave surging toward the far bank. A squadron of tugboats blasts their whistles and quickly nudge the great vessel alongside the fitting-out dock.

The dignitaries retire to a celebratory luncheon at the Cape Fear Country Club. Workers like Elverton Shands, who was trained as a tank tester at Newport News before returning to the shipyard for the launching of the *Vance*, head for home.

Scarcely twenty-four hours later, he is upstairs listening to the radio. "It was the Washington Redskins and the Bears game," he recalls. A newscaster interrupts the game to report that Japanese Forces have attacked Pearl Harbor. "Well, I knew my father was in the Navy. . . . And I came downstairs and I said 'Daddy, where's Pearl Harbor?' " His father tells him.[11]

Now, the Liberty Armada will be sailing into a world war.

The ships launched on the Cape Fear are considered among the best and most efficiently built vessels of their time, but on April 16, 1946, the last ship slides down the ways—the SS *Santa Isabel*. The North Carolina Shipbuilding Company shutters its operation—and releases most of its twenty-five thousand workers.

Local boosters, reinforced by the new N.C. State Ports Authority's attorney, former Gov. Broughton, want the shipyard to remain an independent, permanent feature on the Cape Fear—a yard specializing in the overhaul and modernization of Liberty- and Victory-class ships. Part of the site would be developed into a modern state deepwater port—planned but never realized after the First World War.

But the boosters don't reckon with the scheme of the parent company, Newport News, to prevent postwar competition with its own yard in Virginia. With the submarine menace gone, demand for new merchant "bottoms" falls off sharply. The Maritime Commission accedes to Newport News, designates the Wilmington shipyard one of four reserve facilities: the yard will remain closed, to be reactivated again only in the event of a national emergency.

After almost five years of active politicking and negotiation by the state's congressional delegation and other proponents, on November 15, 1949, the state ports authority is granted a fifty-year lease on the northeast section of the yard—the beginning of a true modern port.

The Liberty Ships at last retire from the high seas, but the port they made possible remains.

Earl Scruggs (second from right) made a name for himself in the earliest days of bluegrass after he hit the road with Bill Monroe and his band.

CHAPTER

SOUNDTRACK
OF THE
DECADE

For more than a decade, the big swing bands like Kay Kaiser's Kollege of Musical Knowledge out of Chapel Hill have been touring the cities and resorts, playing hotel ballrooms. Now they follow the troops overseas to makeshift USOs on bases in Europe and the far-flung Pacific islands. Back home, a new sound is fast sweeping the hinterlands: with deep roots in the textile mill culture of the North Carolina Piedmont, "hillbilly music" by mill-hand bands such as the Briarhoppers is being broadcast on high-wattage radio.

Earl Scruggs is a friendly country boy raised on a farm in Flint Hill. He plays music—guitar, like most of his family—but especially the banjo left by his father, who died when Scruggs was four.

Scruggs discovered what would become his signature

technique when he was ten. He was shut in his bedroom alone, fresh from a "fuss" with his brother Horace, trying to play a song called "Ruben." He'd been playing it for awhile. "And all of a sudden, I realized I was picking with three fingers. And that excited me to no end." He burst out of the room yelling, "I've got it! I've got it! I can play with three fingers!" A week later, when he was still playing the same tune with the same roll, Horace kidded him: Was that was all he could play?[1]

Soon afterward, Scruggs buys himself a Montgomery Ward banjo for $10.95. Later he trades up to a Gibson. Some players have been picking with thumb, index, and middle finger since before the Civil War, but Scruggs takes the style into overdrive, sounding six to eight notes per second in lightning-fast melodic rolls—three-note rolls crowded into two-beat bars.

He graduates Boiling Springs High School in 1942. Instead of being drafted into the war, Scruggs remains at home to support his widowed mother, maintaining and repairing the great spinning machinery at Lily Mills in nearby Shelby for forty cents an hour.

On weekends, he drives his 1936 Chevy across the state line to Spartanburg, South Carolina, to watch Don Reno play his banjo on WSPA's live radio show. Like a number of other players, Reno plays an up-tempo three-finger picking style rather than an old-time clawhammer style.

Soon Scruggs, too, is playing "hillbilly music" on a live radio show in Spartanburg, with the Morris Brothers. But he's still working full-time at the mill. His mother, Lula Ruppe Scruggs, urges him to quit and devote himself to music. He takes her advice and lands a spot with Lost John Miller and the Allied Kentuckians—based in Knoxville, Tennessee, but always on the road—and a gig on the radio that pays fifty dollars per week. Before a performance, he dries out and tensions the banjo head by holding it near the heat of a light bulb—so each note jumps off the strings with a dazzling crispness, clean and distinct.

In generations past, hometown players would entertain their families and friends on porches, in living rooms, in a neighbor's barn or store. The ambitious ones traveled the "kerosene circuit"—playing unelectrified school auditoriums, empty tobacco warehouses, and fairground sheds.

But radio is changing all that—fast.

As electrification lights up rural farmsteads, the radio becomes a fixture in even remote homes. North Carolina begins the decade with twenty-five stations and keeps adding more.

In the early 1920s, a radio cost more than $200—a fortune for a working family. By 1940, a tabletop radio can be bought for as little as six dollars. By mid-decade, rural North Carolina is linked to the national music scene—and contributing significantly to it.

In 1922, WBT Charlotte went on the air as the first fully licensed station south of Washington, D.C. Initially it broadcast just two hours a day at 100 watts. In 1941, the Carter Family joins a robust programming schedule of "hillbilly music" and local string bands. From 5:15 until 6:15 every morning, A. P. and his wife, Sara, her cousin Maybelle, and Maybelle's young daughter June perform a live radio show—sponsored by Kolorbak Hair Dye and Peruna Tonic.

By 1944, WBT is the only station in the Southeast to broadcast twenty-four hours a day, featuring Arthur "Guitar Boogie" Smith and his Crackerjacks and gospel singers such as the Golden Gate Quartet and the Southland Jubilee Singers on popular live shows such as Carolina Hayride and the Crazy Barn Dance.

WPAQ begins broadcasting on Groundhog Day, 1948, from its brick-and-timber home in Mount Airy as the "Voice of the Blue Ridge." The man behind the enterprise is Ralph Epperson. Born in nearby Ararat, Virginia, he is not a musician, but he sees that commercial radio is threatening to completely transform the music he loves.

His pledge to the Federal Communications Commission is simple: he will promote the region's long, rich tradition of old-time, bluegrass, and gospel music. Every Saturday, a parade of local players and singers takes the stage for the Merry-Go-Round—broadcast live first from the studio, then, when crowds overwhelm the modest space, from the Pick Theater in downtown Mount Airy.

Tommy Jarrell, who operates a road grader for the state highway department, lights up the crowd with his syncopated fiddling, embellishing melodic notes with sliding flourishes. Another local fiddler, Benton Flippen, also plays a similar rhythmic "round peak" old-time style.

The Merry-Go-Round also draws names that are already becoming legends: the Carter family; Mac Wiseman, known as "the Voice with a Heart"; Bill and Charlie Monroe, who for a time hosted a daily show on WBT in Charlotte; and Lester Flatt and his young banjo-busting partner, Earl Scruggs.

By 1945, Scruggs is playing on WNOX in Knoxville and WSM in Nashville. There he auditions for Bill Monroe and his Blue Grass Boys, the top band in the South—including Lester Flatt, guitarist and lead singer.

Flatt is impressed: "It was so different! I had never heard that kind of banjo picking. We had been limited but Earl made all the difference in the world." Scruggs debuts with the band on December 8, 1945, on the Grand Ole Opry, broadcast live from the Ryman Auditorium—the premier stage in America for traditional and country music.[2]

Combined with Cedric Rainwater's bouncy acoustic bass, Chubby Wise's keening fiddle, Monroe's energetic mandolin, and Flatt's slick, single-note flat-picking, Scruggs's hard-driving banjo style completes a rollicking, high lonesome sound that has been forming for years out of old-time tunes, traditional Celtic ballads, sacred music, and Appalachian fiddling—soon to be called "bluegrass" after Monroe's band. The Ryman audience erupts with furious applause, and Scruggs's banjo picking resonates in homes across the country as the signature of the new music.

The Blue Grass Boys crisscross the country, usually by automobile, playing packed shows at auditoriums and movie houses, often multiple shows in the same day—"bicycling" between one theater and another in between feature films. The schedule is grueling, the pay modest—especially after Scruggs pays for his own hotel room and meals. Three years later, weary of life on

The Foggy Mountain Boys: guitarist Lester Flatt and banjo player Earl Scruggs.

the road, he returns home to North Carolina. A few weeks later, Lester Flatt joins him, and they form the Foggy Mountain Boys.

Four years after his Opry debut, on December 11, 1949, Scruggs and his band lean into the mics at the Herzog Studio in Cincinnati. Scruggs jumps off into a lightning-fast tune he calls "Foggy Mountain Breakdown"—a frantic three-chord romp of sixteenth-note rolls at breakneck speed all up and down the neck of his banjo that repeats thirteen times and lasts just two minutes and forty seconds.

Thelonious Monk

Nobody has ever played anything like it—and it will outlive the man who wrote and performed it, to be played more than a million times for public audiences. Earl Scruggs has become the most famous banjo player in America. He is twenty-five years old.

Thelonious Monk Jr. is the grandson of Hinton Monk, who grew up a slave on the Willis Cole plantation in Johnston County, overrun by eighty-five thousand troops during the Battle of Bentonville.

Thelonious Monk Jr. is born in Rocky Mount in the wake of a fierce storm on October 17, 1917, and is deliberately named— Thelonious is the Latin form of St. Tillo, a seventh-century Benedictine missionary who was taken into slavery. His parents, Thelonious Sr. and Barbara, share the collective family memory of slavery and the Klan violence of Reconstruction, and they place a high value on freedom.

After his father loses his job with the Atlantic Coast Line Railroad in 1922 and becomes ill, his mother makes a bold move: she determines to raise her three children in New York, out of the segregated South. She leaves her husband behind in North Carolina.

Thelonious Monk doesn't have a formal piano lesson until he is eleven, but he begins learning the instrument much earlier. "I learned how to read before I took lessons," he says later, "watching my sister practice her lessons over her shoulder."[3]

One of his early teachers is Alberta Simmons, a veteran of the speakeasies around the city, where she plays ragtime and "stride" piano—a Harlem jazz variation of ragtime in which the left hand alternates a single bass note with a full chord as the right hand plays the melody.

Monk gets his start playing rent parties for three dollars a night. He learns to play fast rolls up and down the keyboard, to add "decorations" to the melody, and masters all the jazz standards. Even as a teenager, he starts writing the songs he will later record ("Round Midnight," "Ruby My Dear") and distilling his raucous party piano playing into a distinctive bare-bones style—deceptively simple, something like pure melodic form. Then he introduces occasional jarring dissonant chords that sound wrong but actually play off the melody and accent it, somehow containing it in the empty space inside the runs and chords. His playing is full of surprising moments—even to himself—and audiences start to recognize him with just a few bars. He's breaking apart the tunes and putting them back together in musical phrases that are both familiar and strange. People don't just listen—they laugh and nod along and even call out his name.

In 1941, Monk lands a gig that puts him on stage with a round-robin of the best jazz musicians in New York—he becomes house piano player at Minton's Playhouse in the Cecil Hotel, earning only about thirty dollars a week. But it's a steady gig. He's twenty-three years old, rail-thin and clean-cut, peering at the piano keys through eyeglasses, and, like most of the other musicians, dressed in a snazzy pin-striped suit.

Night after night, he sits in with any player who can keep up with him—many of them, like him, talented unknowns. But soon the jams include bigger names like Charlie Parker and Dizzy Gillespie. Monk hits it off with Kenny "Klook-Mop" Clarke, the drummer who serves as house bandleader. Like Monk, Clarke specializes in offbeat accents, letting the bass player keep the rhythm, and using the drums to add surprise and interest.[4]

Monk plays familiar music in an idiom all his own. "I like the whole song, melody and chord structure, to be different," Monk explains. "I make up my own chords and melodies."[5]

Thoughtful critics recognize this for what it is: a studied, inspired rebellion against rules and structures of the past. A will toward freedom.

While Thelonious Monk is jamming on 118th St., down on 56th Street, in 1943, another Monk takes over as musical director of Le Ruban Bleu, a fashionable supper club: Julius Monk. Like Thelonious, he, too, plays jazz piano. He, too, hails from North Carolina. Julius Monk's great-grandfather, Archibald Monk, once "owned" John Jack Monk—Thelonious Monk's great-grandfather. Now the two great-grandsons—one white and the other Black—are listed sequentially on the roll of Local 802 of the American Federation of Musicians.

John Coltrane

John William Coltrane is born in Hamlet in 1926. His parents, a tailor and a seamstress, soon move the family to High Point. Coltrane is known as a shy, quiet, smart boy. In fifth grade, he writes an essay about Marian Anderson, the opera singer, and admires the poetry of Langston Hughes. He is a model student, salutatorian at his grammar school graduation. He is also just discovering music—his first instrument is the alto horn; after that, the clarinet. His mother is an amateur piano player, and his father plays violin and ukulele, but not publicly.

Eight months before he starts at William Penn High School— also known as High Point Normal and Industrial—Coltrane and his family are devastated by the deaths of his father, his grandparents, and an uncle. Brooding and distracted, Coltrane disappears into his music. He practices incessantly, obsessively. He slacks off on his studies.

Without his father's income, the family falls on hard times, and his mother, Alice, decides to move north to Philadelphia to find work, leaving her son alone to finish high school.

Meanwhile Coltrane takes up the alto sax and plays in the small school band. His bandmates are impressed that he can play even difficult tunes by ear, with no need for sheet music. And he seems to carry his school-issued sax everywhere, playing at all hours, endlessly practicing. He graduates in 1943, voted "most musical," and moves to Philadelphia with friends from High Point.

In Philadelphia, his mother buys him his first—used—saxophone. He plays constantly, upsetting the quiet of his apartment building and, to keep the peace, is finally allowed to practice in a nearby church.

Near Coltrane's apartment, an after-hours joint called the Woodbine Club hosts regular weekend jams for local musicians—joined from time to time by big players fresh from gigs around town: Lester Young, Coleman Hawkins, Duke Ellington.

Coltrane thrives on the scene. For the first time, he hears Charlie Parker play—and meets him after the gig. He writes later, "The first time I heard Bird play, it hit me right between the eyes."[6]

By 1945, he has his own trio, but his gigging is interrupted when he is inducted into the navy. At Pearl Harbor he joins an all-Black navy band called the Melody Masters, playing swing with the band but learning the fine points of bebop in his spare time. Once out of the service, he tours with Eddie "Cleanhead" Vinson, playing tenor sax—and finishes the decade touring with Dizzy Gillespie.

Coltrane becomes a technical virtuoso who develops a style of phrasing that redefines his instrument with the sheer fluid density of the riffs. Ahead of him still are battles with alcohol and drug addiction, but his pioneering work wins out. He incorporates idioms from Africa, Asia, and Latin America. He changes jazz forever.

Coltrane performs one of his most memorable concerts with the Thelonious Monk Quartet at Carnegie Hall in 1957. Among the other performers sharing the bill are Billie Holiday, Ray Charles, and Dizzy Gillespie. Coltrane dies young—just forty years old. He posthumously wins a Grammy for best improvised jazz solo, a Grammy Lifetime Achievement Award, and a special citation from the Pulitzer Prize Board—recognitions that pale in comparison to his lasting jazz legacy.

In the 1940s, all eyes were on the sky above Fort Bragg. President Truman paid a visit to the Sandhills to see paratroopers of the 82nd Airborne demonstrate new techniques.

CHAPTER

HOME
OF THE
AIRBORNE

When war comes, formerly remote places take on a new importance. A rugged landscape encompassing three hundred square miles of longleaf pine, wire grass, and wetlands northwest of Fayetteville becomes one of the most crucial training and staging grounds for the U.S. Army: Camp Bragg, named for Confederate General Braxton Bragg.

The post is established in 1918 to train six artillery brigades—sixteen thousand soldiers and almost six thousand horses and mules to haul the guns. The army purchases the land from local families for about $6 million. The sandy soil makes it poor farmland—for thousands of years, Tuscarora and other Native bands traversed the coastal wilderness, leaving behind Clovis spear points, arrowheads, and pottery shards at hundreds of sites, none of which shows more than transitory use.[1]

But the piney sandhills region is a perfect place to fire off artillery, far enough from Fayetteville and Southern Pines to the west, served by a reliable rail and road network, and usable in all seasons. Based at nearby Pope Air Field—named for Lt. Harley Pope, who perished that same year, 1918, when his plane ditched in the Cape Fear River while surveying an airmail route to South Carolina—a squadron of Curtiss JN-4D Jenny biplanes patrols for wildfires and, during training, measures the accuracy of artillery fire on the ground. The place remains so wild that pilots are instructed to buzz the grass field before landing to chase off browsing deer.[2]

But by the time the camp is operational, the Great War is over and the War Department, its funding cut, plans to close the base. Camp Bragg's commanding general, Albert J. Bowley, is determined to keep it open. General Bowley is a hard-driving West Point officer, a veteran of the Spanish-American War in the Philippines and the last crucial offensives of the Great War. He fought at St. Mihiel and the Meuse-Argonne and also served as aide-de-camp to Maj. Gen. Frederick Dent Grant, son of the Civil War hero and U.S. president.[3]

He has the support of boosters in Fayetteville, for whom the base has become a significant part of its civic identity. So, on September 30, 1922, it officially becomes *Fort* Bragg—a permanent post.[4]

Now as the nation reels from the attack on Pearl Harbor, the number of troops at Fort Bragg increases from 5,400 to 67,000 in a single year. By war's end, the Fort Bragg complex, including troops at nearby Camp Mackall, will house nearly 100,000 soldiers. And many of those soldiers will prove themselves to be the most elite troops in the world.[5]

In 1895, thirty-odd miles north of the Sandhills in Dunn, a small turpentine-distilling and logging town, William Carey Lee is born. The son of a Civil War veteran, he grows up working in the tobacco and cotton fields, lends a hand at the family hardware store, becomes an avid hunter and outdoorsman, and matures into an independent thinker and physically active young man. At Wake Forest College and later North Carolina State, he signs on for ROTC and plays baseball and football.

When the Great War comes, Lee enlists, leads a platoon and later a company in combat, and is part of the Army of Occupation in Germany. After deciding to make the army his career, he studies tank warfare at Fort Meade and is posted to France for further training in armored warfare. Lee travels extensively in Europe, and in Germany sees for the first time a German parachute regiment in action—dropping from airplanes in a tactic called "vertical envelopment." If an army can place troops in the enemy's rear in one fell swoop, hem them in behind frontal and flanking assaults, the enemy can be routed.

Lee carries the idea home to his new post in Washington, D.C., where he becomes a champion of developing airborne troops. Gen. George C. Marshall, chief of staff of the army, is also intrigued by the idea of airborne troops, as is President Franklin Roosevelt. Lee, then a lieutenant colonel, is summoned to brief the president, and in March 1940, he is put in command of the Provisional Parachute Group at Fort Benning, Georgia. He recruits volunteers from the 29th Infantry to form a Parachute Test Platoon of unmarried men in prime physical condition with at least two years of experience in the army. "We wanted them cocky, self-confident, aggressive, and proud," he says, "but above all we insisted on good discipline."[6]

His first makeshift uniform for the new unit consists of mechanic's overalls (his prototype pair borrowed from his own brother), high-top leather tanker's boots, and a Riddell football helmet like the one he wore in college. The uniform evolves with experience to feature a special jacket modeled on those worn by German airborne troops, an equipment harness,

Paratrooper floats to the ground at Fort Bragg during a jump
in honor of St. Michael, the patron saint of paratroopers.
© Andrew Craft – USA TODAY NETWORK

baggy trousers with cargo pockets, and a steel helmet with a chin cup and strap. The high lace-up boots with baggy pants tucked into them become a distinguishing emblem of pride for airborne troops.[7]

On a jump in November 1941, Lee breaks his back, and when the stunning news of the Pearl Harbor attack comes over the radio, he is still recuperating in an upper body cast. But the success of the original test platoon has led to the creation of two full airborne divisions of ten thousand men each, supported by engineers and artillery: the 101st and the 82nd—plus glider-borne units—all under the command of Lee, now a brigadier general. In April 1942, the units from Fort Benning and Fort Claiborne in Louisiana are consolidated under the Airborne Command at Fort Bragg. Among Lee's handpicked officers are Matthew Ridgway, James Gavin, and Maxwell Taylor. Ridgway and Gavin both go on to command the 82nd Airborne and Taylor the division's artillery. Lee commands the 101st.

The patron saint of the airborne troops is Michael the Archangel, the winged warrior who stands with his heel atop Satan, poised to impale him with the tip of his spear.[8]

Fort Bragg grows at an astonishing rate. Dirt roads are paved, as are the landing fields at Pope. Railroad tracks running into the base carry trainloads of lumber, galvanized metal sheeting, and concrete. Cranes and forklifts off-load the cargo alongside the track, and crews scramble to retrieve it. The building crews work in a continuous, synchronized fashion to get the work done—fast.[9]

Nearly three thousand new wooden buildings spring up—barracks and mess halls, headquarters offices and classrooms—post-and-beam construction of the most basic kind, spartan and utilitarian, with galvanized metal roofs and walls.

After pouring concrete flooring slabs, a crew can erect an entire building in as little as thirty minutes. In this manner, four complexes of barracks are built—lined in straight avenues each nearly a mile long and a quarter-mile broad.[10]

But even with the frenzy of construction, Fort Bragg is not large enough to handle the flood of airborne and other troops assigned to train and stage for overseas deployment. So in 1942, a short distance southwest of Fort Bragg, the army builds a complementary facility with 1,750 buildings to train airborne troops, named Camp Mackall in honor of paratrooper John T. Mackall, who was killed in the assault on Algiers. Like Fort Bragg, it features a companion airfield to launch C-47s, the aircraft that will carry troops to their combat drop zones.

At Fort Bragg and Camp Mackall, paratroopers undergo extraordinarily rigorous physical training; learn gunnery and tactics, map-reading and communication; and practice mock-parachuting from thirty-four-foot-high towers down cables to a landing zone below.

They are trained how to stand in the doorway of the aircraft, static line hooked to the overhead wire, looking at the horizon and never the ground: feet together, bent slightly at the waist, hands steadied against the outside of the open doorway, head bowed onto chest. They are taught to jump six inches up and thirty-six inches out with elbows tucked tight against the body and to let the prop wash carry them away from the plane and open their chute—eighteen men out the door in ten seconds.[11]

Once out the door and airborne under their chutes, they are trained to do the following: Grab the risers and lift their heads to check their canopy and lines to make sure nothing is tangled, that the chute has bloomed open. Then to check for other parachutists, to make sure they don't collide with them and become entangled. As they approach the ground, to press their legs and feet together to avoid cracking their kneecaps together or breaking an ankle. To lower their gear under them so that it lands first and decide whether to hit the ground forward left, forward center, or forward right with knees bent. At the moment of impact—a jolt like jumping off a three-foot high platform—they are to tuck and roll, control their chutes against the wind by grabbing the lines closest to the ground, then unharness, gather their weapons, and run to their designated assembly area.

And at last, they make that first jump—the moment of truth. It will take five successful jumps to earn each man the coveted silver wings of the airborne. If a paratrooper freezes in the doorway, he will likely be reassigned out of the airborne. Remarkably, very few ever freeze. And because they have been trained to hold onto the outside of the fuselage, never the inside, if a man freezes on a combat jump, he can be easily pushed out by the jumpmaster behind him.

As one veteran paratrooper puts it, "You're so hyped, they've got you so pumped up, you just go. It's the second jump that gets you thinking." And no matter how many jumps they make, it's always a thrill.[12]

Fort Bragg becomes home to all five U.S. Army Airborne divisions: the 101st, the 82nd, the 11th, the 13th, and the 17th. The first Black parachute regiment—the 555th, or "Triple Nickel"—undergoes training in parachutes and gliders. Conventional units, including the 9th and 100th infantry divisions, crowd the training areas and parade grounds. The artillery ranges resound with live fire as tens of thousands of gunners learn their trade. The 2nd Armored Division moves in.[13]

In September 1943, General Lee is ordered to England along with his airborne division to prepare for the invasion of occupied Europe. Approaching fifty years of age, he trains for ten months alongside his troops in the 101st, even on their twenty-five-mile hikes. "This is better than plowing a mule on my farm in Dunn," he quips.

But the long, grueling seven-day weeks take their toll. In February 1944, Lee suffers a major heart attack and must return home to Walter Reed Hospital to recover. He misses the invasion jump.

Still, the airborne troops he once dreamed of are a reality. The pathfinders of the 101st "Screaming Eagles" are the first to land in occupied France in the early hours of D-Day—June 6, 1944—followed by waves of paratroopers clearing the way for the seaborne assaults on Omaha and Utah beaches. Meanwhile the 82nd—already veterans of night jumps into Sicily in 1943— drops twelve thousand parachute and glider troops to capture vital causeways across the wetlands behind the beaches and engages in sustained combat for more than a month without relief. From his home in Dunn, Lee listens to the welcome news on the radio.[14]

The cover of *Newsweek* magazine for June 19, 1944, features a photograph of a paratrooper in midair, having just cleared the jump door. The caption reads: "Air Invader: He Is the 1944 Invasion Spearhead."

After the war, Fort Bragg becomes the permanent home of the 82nd Airborne. Veterans return home with war brides from Germany and elsewhere and settle in Fayetteville, often in the same neighborhoods.

The quality of the men who train at Fort Bragg is often extraordinary. Many go on to professional careers as doctors, engineers, teachers, and scientists. They become community leaders, contribute in every area of its civic and cultural life, and justify Gen. Bowley's stubborn conviction that Fort Bragg should remain open—from now on as the home of the Airborne.

Residents of Bryson City
hadn't seen many hurricanes
before August 1940. Those
who survived the destruction
left in the storm's wake
surely hoped they'd never
see another one like it.

CHAPTER

THE
DELUGE

The Southeast Hurricane barrels into Beaufort, South Carolina, on August 11, 1940, as a Category 2 storm with sustained winds of eight-five miles per hour. It moves inland into Georgia, then unpredictably hooks north along the Appalachians and churns into North Carolina from the west, bringing five days of unrelenting torrential rainfall.[1]

The hurricane is the latest in a series of storms that already have dumped more than twenty-one inches of rain on the mountain region during the month of August. Downtown Boone is submerged in muddy water, rising by the hour, as eight inches of rain fall in just forty-eight hours. Elsewhere, the water comes all at once in torrents.[2]

Just east of Boone, and southeast of Deep Gap and the partially completed Blue Ridge Parkway, water is sluicing down steep mountainsides into the two prongs of Stony Fork Creek—toward the home of Zeb Greene, one of many Greenes living in the small, scattered community of Stony Fork. Here, houses perch on stone foundations along creeks in the low, flat ground between hills, often with small gristmills. Zeb's two-story wooden house was built by his father, David, in the 1850s on a foundation of chestnut logs laid on creek and pasture rocks. Zeb's brother Elster lives within hailing distance.[3]

At home with Zeb are other relatives who are stranded there by the rising creek as night falls: Worth and Lucy Greene and their one-and-a-half-year-old daughter, Betty, and Lucy's first cousin Nina Todd, fifteen—a bright-eyed junior at Happy Valley High School in Peterson. She made the honor roll and earned a medal inscribed, "An All Around Best Girl." Just last night, Nina harmonized with her cousin Beulah Greene while singing the hymn "I Would Rather Have Jesus" at the Stony Fork revival, cut short because of the violent storms.

The howling early darkness is split by eerie flashes of lightning along the course of the flood and a weird, low, electric light. And over the slamming rush of the rain can be heard another sound: a rumble like thunder erupting in punctuated bursts, then sustained in a long, trembling roar. It is the sound of mountainsides falling—great landslides hundreds of feet wide, the overburden of soil saturated by continuous rain and loosened by the big timber outfits that have clear-cut the old-growth forest, whose roots once held soil to bedrock. Now the ridges break away in massive avalanches of earth, rock, and timber weighing thousands of tons and moving as fast as forty miles per hour.[4]

Because the slides erupt out of the darkness, their victims can't see them coming, can hear the earthshaking roar only when it is too late.

In the southeastern quadrant of Watauga County alone, more than six hundred landslides sweep down into creeks and across roadways, burying houses and other buildings, destroying railroad tracks, cutting off entire communities from the outside world, and killing twelve people. As many as two hundred more slides descend on southern and central Watauga.[5]

By nine o'clock, the rain is lashing at the Greene home in horizontal sheets. Zeb Greene ventures onto the front porch, accompanied by Worth Greene and Nina Todd, to see about moving the hogs to higher ground—in many of the little valleys, anxious farmers are turning out their livestock to fend for themselves. The onrushing wall of water catches the three by surprise and carries away Zeb and Nina. From his front porch, Elster Greene can hear his brother's panicked cries, but he is powerless to rescue him. Worth leaps from the porch into a nearby cedar tree and waits out the night there as the flood swirls below in the pitch darkness.

Worth's wife, Lucy, carries the baby, Betty, upstairs, and the two survive the long tumultuous night. In the morning, a foot and a half of mud and water covers the floors of the ruined house. Betty is reminded of that calamitous night her whole life. She recalls, "Mama felt guilty the rest of her life that Nina, her first cousin, died, because she and daddy had gone to get Nina to come sing at the revival at Stony Fork Baptist Church."[6]

Nina Todd's body is found, half-buried in river mud and sand, more than twenty miles away, not far from Zeb's body—both carried clear across the Yadkin River by the force of the flood. Nina is so mangled that no one is allowed to view her remains. She is identified by her wristwatch and the belt she was known to be wearing.

Mrs. Ivery C. Greene, a neighbor from Deep Gap who survives, ventures into the flood-ravaged community to collect their stories and composes an astonishingly intimate chronicle of the disaster. She writes, "The flood came like a thief in the night—suddenly, unexpected by everyone."[7]

The house of Ivery's father, John D. Cook, where she grew

up alongside three sisters and seven bothers, is demolished by the raging flood of water and mud, along with most of the outbuildings and the orchard of apple and plum trees. Luckily, the family has been evacuated, but a prized heirloom—a one-hundred-year-old spinning wheel—is destroyed. Ivery writes, "Now it is a place of sadness and desolation, a pleasant spot in memory only. In my mind's eye, I can see it now, the home as it was when we happy children gathered around the fireside with mother and father; when we sang together in the comfortable living room."[8]

Elsewhere in Deep Gap, another tragedy is playing out—four homes within half a mile of each other are crushed by landslides. At the home of Andrew and Eliza Greene, the family has just finished evening prayers. The avalanche of earth and trees tears the house from its foundation and tumbles it end over end three times, demolishing it. Their neighbors, the Verdie Greene family, witness the calamity, as Ivery chronicles soon after: "The whole family were standing on the front porch listening to the roaring of the waters and watching the nearby streams rise higher and higher every minute. They heard the screams of those who went down to their deaths."[9]

Andrew, forty-six, is carried three miles, and his body is deposited near a large oak tree. "His right hand held onto a piece of an iron bedpost in a death grip. He had been standing near the iron bed that stood in his living room when the house started to crumble, and it is thought that he grasped the bedpost as the house overturned and was instantly killed."[10]

His wife, Eliza, is caught fast in a drift of logs, sand, and debris, in water up to her hips. She struggles free, losing her shoes, and climbs atop a higher drift for safety. "There I sat all night," she recalls, "calling for help and hoping someone would rescue me."

Her youngest son, B. L., age seven, can hear her calling. He was asleep in an upstairs bedroom when the slide struck and regains consciousness caught in a clog of debris fifty yards downstream from his mother, dazed and bruised, his face caked with mud, but otherwise unharmed. In the morning, he crosses a swollen creek on a downed tree to reach his uncle's house and walks in on breakfast. "No, I wasn't a bit afraid," he says. "Didn't even cry either. There were pretty little lights around me all night and I could hear mama, not far above me, calling for somebody."[11]

Eliza and Andrew's son Hooper, nineteen, is caught up on a bush and holds on through the night. He hears his sister Velma Lea, fourteen, carried past him screaming. His other two sisters, Creola, sixteen, and Vernita, twelve, also drown. Their mother, Eliza, is not allowed to view their broken and disfigured bodies. She complains, "If I could have seen them and but touched their faces and hands one more time, I could have stood the loss better." Three days later, four caskets are lined up at the foot of the pulpit of their church as the choir softly sings the girls' favorite hymn, "I Feel Like Traveling On." In bright sunshine, the three brown-haired, blue-eyed daughters are laid to rest with their father in a single common grave heaped with flowers.[12]

Not far from Andrew and Eliza Greene's house, Bessie Greene, a widow with seven children—three girls and two boys at home—is awakened by the crashing down of the brick chimney onto the roof. Her house is swept off its foundation and carried three hundred yards, where it fetches up against a downed sugar maple and a pile of stones. Bessie Greene and her children flee the shattered house but are caught between a landslide and a flooding creek. Joe, the eldest boy, says, "It looks as if we are going to be destroyed any way we can go." They find a path around the slide, slog through mud and water to the home of Lawrence Greene—who suffers a heart attack upon learning that his two brothers, Andrew and Millard, have both died in the flood. He is trapped in his house until the waters recede the next day and they can take him to the hospital.[13]

At the foot of the Fire Scalds—high-bluffed mountains near Deep Gap—two filling stations owned by Odis Watson and Guy Carlton are overwhelmed by the torrent and swept away along with Carlton's house. Twelve people are caught by the water and the body of one, a nine-year-old boy named Johnnie Greene, comes to rest miles downstream. By the heroic efforts of Watson and Carlton, the others are rescued. They carry the injured, bruised, and broken, to Watauga Hospital in Boone. One of them is Carlton's mother-in-law, Martha Carrol—both legs broken and chest crushed. She does not survive.[14]

Another victim in a different locale, William Townsend, sixty-eight, is washed nearly fifty miles and, when the flood abates, is discovered wedged onto a cliff near Elizabethton, Tennessee. Some victims are just plain swept away, never to be found.[15]

The *Sylva Herald & Ruralite* records other deaths, those of the McCall family of Canada in Jackson County. As a landslide engulfs their house, it "carried Mrs. McCall across the raging creek where she caught the top of a tree and saved herself." The body of the McCalls' five-year-old son washes up on an island near Bryson City—almost sixty miles away. But Albert McCall and the couple's other child are never found.

Near Grandfather Mountain, the cab crew of Engine 9 is flagged down as they are heading up the long grade to Cranberry Gap. They back the train downhill toward town, but another washout forces them to abandon their locomotive. There will be no more trains running on that line—and the great flood has cut off rail service to Boone for good.[16]

Other western counties suffer as well. The *Skyland Post* of Ashe County reports that "nine bridges over the New River in the county were either partly or totally washed away, and several bridges over creeks were moved by the terrific force of fast running water."

At Lansing, Big Horse Creek overflows and floods the Norfolk and Western railroad station in surging water four feet deep. It takes more than a month to repair the tracks and restore service. Some thirty homes and fifty barns are swept away, and more than twice as many homes are damaged. The crop fields of as many as a thousand farms are inundated.[17]

Flood waters overwhelm the power station at the Hamby Dam at Warrensville, washing part of it away.[18]

The French Broad wipes out the bridge at Marshall. Along the rampaging Tuckasegee, wooden bridges are swept away, and so is the steel span at Dillsboro. The Watauga—cresting like the Yadkin at six feet above the record set by the 1916 flood—washes

The Tuckasegee River topped its banks in Cullowhee in August 1940, wiped out the Old Cullowhee Road bridge, and destroyed a lumber company's rail spur.

out bridges at Cove Creek and Valle Crucis. The torrents of rain turn Grandfather Mountain into a gigantic waterfall, and the Watauga River sweeps through the settlement there, carrying most of it away. The power plant downriver at Shulls Mills—the first in the county—is wrecked.[19]

Highway 421 to Wilkesboro is cut. On Route 18, a bus from Lenoir bound for North Wilkesboro is knocked on its side by the flood sweeping across the roadway. A man, a woman, her nine-year-old son, and the driver manage to escape and wade to safety.[20]

South of Grandfather Mountain in Caldwell County, in the rugged, remote Pisgah National Forest, Wilson Creek careens through its steep-walled gorge with alarming force toward the small community of Mortimer. The town was hastily constructed in 1904 to house about eight hundred employees of the Ritter Lumber Company timber and sawmill operation, plus a textile mill.

Ritter shut down its timber operation in 1916, after Wilson Creek flooded and wiped out the narrow-gauge railroad it used to haul out its milled logs—but not before clear-cutting old-growth timber between Wilson and Steel creeks and, in the process stripping the mountainsides of the cover that holds the earth in place.

By 1940, Mortimer includes homes, a smithy, a school, a church, a movie house, even a hotel—the Laurel Inn. It is also home to Civilian Conservation Corps Camp F-5, which takes over the warehouse buildings. Then on August 13, Wilson Creek engulfs the creekside town with a flood cresting at ninety-four feet—and the town never recovers.[21]

It goes down in history as the Great Flood of 1940, but it's really many floods: Of the Watauga, Yadkin, Little Tennessee, Tuckasegee, New, and French Broad Rivers. Of Stony Fork Creek and Linville Creek and Swift Ford Branch and a hundred other bold creeks in Watauga, Ashe, Wilkes, Haywood, Caldwell, and other mountain counties.

It is a great deluge not just of water but also of earth—as if the mountains themselves are dissolving into a cold lava clotted with boulders and stumps and green trees and the wooden bones of broken barns and houses—and too many bodies of innocents caught unawares in the dark of night, carried off from their homes by this rampaging creature of storms, this devastating legacy of clear-cut mountainsides, this nightmare come true.

Unto These Hills tells the story of the Cherokee, their achievements, and their sacrifices. The Mountainside Theatre has hosted the production for almost seventy years.

CHAPTER

LAND
OF
BLUE SMOKE

For the Eastern Band of Cherokee Indians, the mountains are sacred and eternal. The land is majestic and beautiful—also rugged and remote. Surviving and prospering in such vertical country has been the challenge of generations. They call their mountain home Land of Blue Smoke.[1]

The sovereign nation, which encompasses nearly one hundred square miles in Jackson and Swain counties at the eastern gateway to the newly formed Great Smoky Mountains National Park, has a proud and stubborn legacy. In 1838, the U.S. government force-marched more than sixteen thousand Cherokees west to Oklahoma from their ancestral lands in Georgia, Florida, Alabama, Tennessee, and the Carolinas. Along the Trail of Tears, some four thousand died.[2]

But the Qualla Cherokees, native to the mountains of western North Carolina, argued successfully that they had severed ties with the Cherokee Nation by the Treaty of 1819 and therefore were exempt from the removal order. They refused to leave their home, the main settlement of which was Qualla Town—now the town of Cherokee.[3]

The heart of their nation remains the Qualla Boundary, purchased by tribal members during the 1840s and 1850s. Though federally protected, it was never really a reservation by the usual definition—though it is called such—because the land never belonged to the U.S. government. In 1940, about 2,200 tribal members live here.[4]

The 1930s have been a time of hardship. Asian blight has nearly wiped out the great forests of chestnut trees on the Qualla Boundary, and timber harvesting has fallen off. Farming, always difficult in such steep country even in the best of times, can't fully support enough families—only about 5 percent of Cherokee land is arable. Also, much of the Boundary has been hunted out, and it's hard to bag even squirrels and woodchucks for the supper pot.[5]

Some small farmers enlist in the Civilian Conservation Corps-Indian Division (CCC-ID). Instead of living in camps, the 150 Cherokee CCC-ID workers remain on their farms and work rotating shifts of two weeks per month in nearby Great Smoky Mountains National Park—cutting trails, building roads and bridges, sawing trees, constructing shelters, patrolling for forest fires—supervised by Chief Jarrett Jaldijula Bythe, grandson of Chief Nimrod Jarrett Smith, in his capacity as subforeman. The rotation is designed to spread out the wages—fifteen dollars per month—over as many men as possible. By 1938, cuts in the CCC-ID budget have thinned their number to just twenty-five.[6]

And on the tail of the Depression comes a blow from nature. On February 20, 1940, Camp Superintendent Clyde M. Blair writes to the Commissioner of Indian Affairs, "During the two months just past, the Cherokee Indian Reservation has experienced its most severe winter in fifty-one years." Temperatures have dipped to twenty below zero. "As a result of this subnormal temperature," he continues, "the Indians have suffered greatly from loss of foodstuffs. Canned fruit and vegetables, potatoes and other root crops have frozen. This has all meant that a greater number than ever before have needed assistance in the way of labor on the CCC and other work projects." Thus he cannot cut his winter payroll, the usual practice. "Since there is not a man on the CCC roll that does not need the work any reduction in the roll would work a serious hardship on the enrollees involved."[7]

The Cherokees have kept their beloved mountains, but the mountains are losing Cherokee men to outside wage work in factories and steel mills. The buildup for war accelerates the exodus: about two dozen men leave to work at Fort Bragg and another 260 are hired on to build the Fontana Dam on the Little Tennessee River not far from Robbinsville. Others sign on as mule skinners during the construction of the Cheoah Dam for ALCOA. There is just no steady livelihood to be had for too many on the Qualla Boundary.[8]

The opening of the national park promised a new boom closer to home from tourists keen to discover Cherokee culture, but this anticipated boom has hardly begun before the war brings rationing of gas and rubber tires, and the parade of automobiles stops.

And roads are sorely lacking. One road in particular has been the cause of much of the division within the tribe: the Blue Ridge Parkway—the last unfinished fifteen miles of which is planned to pass through the Qualla Boundary.

The Parkway is a federal project, so claiming a right-of-way through a federally protected reservation of a federally recognized tribe should not be difficult. But because the Cherokees own their land as a corporation under a state charter granted

Construction of the Blue Ridge Parkway from Soco Gap to Big Witch Gap in the early 1940s brings outsiders—and, with them, changes to the Qualla Boundary.

to Chief Nimrod Jarrett Smith in 1889, the lines of jurisdiction are murky.[9]

Furthermore, Harold Ickes, the Secretary of the Interior, has made it clear he won't proceed without the Cherokees' support. In his "Message to the Cherokee Tribe," he writes, "If you do not want the road to be built where the National Park Service desires it to go, it will not be built."[10]

At first, the tribal council votes for approval—the new highway will connect them with Asheville and revive the tourist trade, so it grants a two-hundred-foot-wide right-of-way through the Soco Valley—where the council already plans to build a road. When the council learns that the proposed right-of-way is one thousand feet wide, they rescind their approval. Such a broad swath of land would claim nearly the entire valley, one of the rare flat areas suitable for farming. And no commercial development would be allowed along it—thus no tourist dollars for the tribe.

As the 1940s near, two strong-willed men, raised in the same household, are trying to pull the tribe toward very different futures. To survive these hard times, to keep their homeland inviolate, to provide for the well-being of their people, the Cherokees face some big decisions.

Chief Jarrett Blythe, first elected in 1931, wants the Parkway—and the prosperity it will bring. He is remarkably popular, a handsome, dignified man trusted by Cherokees and whites alike. Clyde Blair calls him "very level-headed," a chief "who has the best interests of the Indians at heart and thoroughly understands the relationship between the Federal Government and the tribe."

But his vice chief, Fred Bauer—elected in 1936 when Blythe is re-elected—becomes his stubborn nemesis. Bauer is the son of A. G. Bauer, the distinguished Raleigh architect who designed the governor's mansion. His mother died shortly after giving birth to him, and his father sent him west to grow up in the home of the boy's great-uncle and aunt, James and Josephine Blythe—Chief Jarrett Blythe's parents. A. G. Bauer committed suicide not long after. Thus Fred Bauer and Jarrett Blythe are raised together.[11]

Bauer graduates Carlisle Indian School and serves in World War I, then goes on to a career teaching in Indian boarding schools in Michigan. He returns to Qualla Boundary with his wife, Catherine, also a teacher. The two launch a spirited crusade against the Parkway, which they brand a new kind of "removal," and the Indian Reorganization Act, known as the "Indian New Deal."

The Indian New Deal marks a turning point in the federal government's Indian policy as administered by the Bureau of Indian Affairs. Previously it encouraged Native Americans to leave reservations for wage work in the cities and discouraged preservation of culture, language, and ritual—and the traditional crafts that supported them. The policy also favored a program of allotment, the term for parceling out tribal land to individuals.

But under John Collier, a former New York social worker appointed by President Franklin D. Roosevelt as Commissioner of Indian Affairs, all of that changes. Acting on authority granted him by the Indian Reorganization Act, Collier encourages tribes to incorporate exactly as the Cherokees have done. This will lead them to act as collectives with considerable bargaining power, to secure financial backing for infrastructure and commercial ventures, to preserve and celebrate their cultures, and to improve the economic fortunes of their members—all the things Chief Blythe is now trying to accomplish, and all the things Bauer is bent on stopping.

Bauer sees assimilation as the only route to social and economic freedom for the Indians. For him, tribalism is just another expression of communism—and a way to keep Indians from succeeding in mainstream America, relegating them to reservations where they can be controlled. He favors the movement gaining momentum in Congress for termination of the federal government's protection and oversight of Native American tribes, which would dissolve their special status and the subsidies they receive and leave every individual to make their own way. So far the Eastern Band under Blythe has successfully resisted termination.

Like Collier, Blythe envisions the best of both worlds for his people: economic progress through tourism carried via the Parkway and preservation of the Cherokee identity and culture through a revival of traditional crafts and ceremonies. An

Tourists in 1945 came to Cherokee Village for an "Indian" experience, which included photos in front of the Cherokee Inn & Trading Post with a Cherokee wearing a very nontraditional headdress.

important bridge between the two will be a revival of an out-door pageant performed with commendable success in 1934 and 1937: *The Spirit of the Great Smokies*. The production foundered due to the logistics of staging 350 actors and dancers—and a nasty fight for control by the Bauer faction.[12]

The rivalry comes to a head in the 1939 election for principal chief when Bauer pits himself against Blythe. But he has badly underestimated the current chief's popularity—Blythe wins more than 80 percent of the vote. Now, in the new decade, Blythe can truly unify the Eastern Cherokee.[13]

Blythe quickly persuades the united council to authorize a Parkway compromise: a ridge route that will bypass Soco Valley, a $40,000 federal payment for the new right-of-way, and a promise to build a commercial highway through the valley.[14]

Meantime, the war won't wait. All Cherokee males between the ages of twenty-one and thirty-five register for the draft. Soon they are serving in integrated units in the army, Army Air Corps, navy, and marines in every theater of war, from Europe to the Pacific islands. Seven are wounded in action. Two are awarded Distinguished Flying Crosses and two others the Silver Star for valor. Twelve Cherokees die in uniform.[15]

When the veterans return home, local registrars deny them the right to vote. Members of the Steve Youngdeer American Legion Post hire an Asheville lawyer to press their case with the U.S. attorney general. Special agents from the FBI show up at Qualla Boundary to investigate their claims while the Cherokee veterans, aided by the district American Legion, lobby legislators and present their case in the newspapers. At last, in 1946, the Swain and Jackson County registrars bow to the pressure and honor the veterans' right to participate in the democracy they fought to preserve.[16]

The next campaign for Chief Blythe and the council is acquisition of the Boundary Tree Tract—nine hundred acres north of Cherokee abutting the new Parkway and Great Smoky Mountains National Park—and by summer 1949 the site of the Cherokees' grand venture into tourism. It's the first commercial enterprise tourists encounter as they leave the park: a Standard Oil gas station, eighteen tourist cabins, a lodge, and a restaurant—all belonging to the tribe.

As construction proceeds on the Boundary Tree project, eleven mountain counties band together to sponsor an outdoor pageant modeled on *The Spirit of the Great Smokies*, originally conceived by Harold W. Foght, the Cherokee agent for the BIA in the 1930s. He wanted to draw visitors to Cherokee and present them with a grand spectacle of history and culture—to educate as much as to impress. To stage the pageant, the counties create the Cherokee Historical Foundation, made up of a mix of whites and Indians. With Highway 19 completed through Soco Valley, county and state money available to fund a new theater, and a federal commitment to build an access road and a parking lot, the time is right.

To accommodate large crowds, the planners envision an outdoor theater, a raised stage surrounded by seating on level ground. Then Samuel Selden offers a different vision. Selden is chairman of the Department of Dramatic Arts and director of the Carolina Playmakers at the University of North Carolina at Chapel Hill (UNC). He successfully directed *The Lost Colony*, Paul Green's long-running outdoor drama staged annually on Roanoke Island, and now is acting as technical adviser to the Cherokee production. The wooded mountainsides inspire him to suggest the idea of an amphitheater built right into the hills. Ross Caldwell, a retired architect and veteran of the Army Corps of Engineers during both world wars, designs such a theater and supervises construction—all pro bono.

A graduate student of Selden's at UNC, Kermit Hunter, scripts an epic story that arcs from the first Cherokee contact with Europeans in 1540 to the Trail of Tears—featuring such historical figures as Sequoyah, who created the written Cherokee language; Junaluska, a legendary chief; and Tsali, revered as a martyr for his people, who helped make it possible for them to remain in their mountain home.

Thus is born *Unto These Hills*—titled for the opening lines of Psalm 121, which are spoken at the beginning of the show: "I will lift up mine eyes unto these hills, from whence cometh my help."[17]

The performance is a theatrical extravaganza, a lively celebration through drama, music, and dance of Cherokee history, culture, and spirit—a tale of betrayal and tragedy, of bravery and sacrifice, of perseverance and reconciliation. It opens in 1950 at the Mountainside Theatre, which features three stages—the biggest eighty feet wide and twenty-five feet deep—and seats nearly three thousand people. It is wildly successful, drawing an audience of more than one hundred thousand for fifty-three performances—paying off its debt in one season and earning a large profit.[18]

Jarrett Blythe is re-elected five times, more than any chief in Cherokee history. Under his leadership, the Eastern Cherokee have made of their mountains a great natural stage on which to present their storied heritage to all who visit the Land of Blue Smoke.

In Tillery, buying supplies cooperatively often meant waiting in line. The successes and struggles of Black farmers across the South were chronicled in 1938 by the Farm Security Administration.

CHAPTER

FIELDS
OF
DREAMS

In 1947, when Gary Grant comes to Tillery, North Carolina, he is a skinny four-year-old kid with knock-knees and a full head of curly hair. Tillery—originally called Tillery's Crossing after a nearby plantation—is a small town in the Roanoke River valley, a remote country of long horizons across table-flat fields of cotton, soybeans, peanuts, and corn. It sits at the crossroads of Route 561 from Halifax and Route 481 from Enfield.

Tillery is a lively place. Seven trains stop here each day—four freights and three passenger trains. A sawmill, cotton gin, and market serve the business of the farmers. On Saturdays, the farmers and sharecroppers converge on the town—its barbershops, post office, bank, restaurants, and stores selling groceries, liquor, appliances, and household goods. As night falls, the dance halls fill up with people ready to shrug off the fatigue of the hard workweek.

On most summer days, the sun beats down relentlessly from a clear blue sky on open fields that are a long way from the sparse shade of distant tree lines, the land drenched in stillness. Other afternoons, the sky is mottled by gray storm clouds, dark bellies full of impending rain that will fall not here but farther east, along the coast.

The Grants have come to rural Halifax County to farm under a program that originated as part of President Franklin D. Roosevelt's New Deal in 1935: the Tillery Farms Resettlement Project. The idea is one of many bold experiments: give tenant-farmer and wageworker families a chance to own their own land.

Gary's father, Matthew Grant, stands over six feet tall, a sturdy man who has been working at the Newport News Shipbuilding and Drydock Company. But he and his wife, Florenza Moore

Gary Grant grew up on a farm in Tillery, graduated from North Carolina College at Durham (now North Carolina Central University), and returned to his hometown to teach elementary school and campaign for civil rights.

Grant, long for a life outside the pent-up city. Gary recalls, "They were just free spirits. They did not like being confined. My father was the youngest of nine children . . . and they were industrious people. My sister describes my father as a dreamer and my mother as a person who helped to make dreams come true."

They have five children and soon adopt an infant boy. Gary is the middle child—with an older sister and brother and a younger sister and brother.

Matthew comes from a landowning family in Potecasi, in Northampton County. Florenza is descended from sharecroppers who lived near Rich Square in the same county. Matthew and Florenza married right out of high school. They are both proud, independent-minded, and self-confident—a spirit they instill in their children. Florenza, who dresses well and projects great dignity, instructs her daughters that just because they live on a farm, they don't have to look like they're working on a farm. When they go into the fields to pick cotton in October, they wear Sunday gloves, to protect their fingers from sharp cotton spurs.

The two parents work as a team, both in family and in business matters. "I think that my parents probably had the best partnership," Gary remembers. "They trusted each other—that was the first thing."[1]

Their attachment to one another is deep and loving. In addition to presiding over the household, Florenza keeps the books and manages other family business enterprises. She is the first woman in the Resettlement to obtain a driver's license, so she cruises around town in her Plymouth, and later a DeSoto. She also drives the local ambulance, delivers crops to market in the family truck, and serves as a midwife for the community.[2]

The Resettlement Administration (RA), which evolves into the Farm Security Administration (FSA), eventually extends credit to 800,000 farming families—nearly 160,000 of them Black. It also purchases millions of acres of farmland

and establishes about sixty planned agricultural communities. Tillery is one of just thirteen such projects reserved for Black farmers. The goal of the RA is for Blacks to comprise 10 percent of its homesteaders—the percentage of Blacks in the farming population.[3]

Not only will this raise their economic prospects and make them self-sufficient; it will also stabilize the larger agricultural economy that suffered such a collapse during the Depression years. During that time, prices dropped even as production faltered in the face of massive droughts in the Midwest and West, supply chains were interrupted, and banks foreclosed on too many farms—or simply refused credit for seed and other essentials.[4]

Originally, Tillery contains a community of white farmers as well. But in 1940, when the ten thousand acres along the Roanoke flood, the federal government moves them to an eight-thousand-acre tract of higher ground west of Halifax. When the fields drain, they are sold on credit to Black families in parcels of forty to sixty acres. But the lucrative tobacco allotments remain with the white farmers. The Black farmers are instructed to grow cotton, soybeans, corn, and peanuts. Among the farms, the government has built a community center and a clinic, and each family pays about two dollars a month for medical coverage.[5]

Outside of town, where the roads turn to graded dirt, Gary recalls, "If you were coming down to Tillery, folks would say, 'You're going to Black Gate,' because this is where the Black resettlement farms started." He himself is descended from enslaved Blacks, white landowners, and Native Americans.[6]

Large equipment such as a pea-picker is collectively owned. The federal government loans money for equipment and operating costs. After a five-year trial tenancy, the FSA lends each family $3,000–$5,000 at 3 percent interest to buy the land and buildings.[7]

For white families, three house types are available: two-story two-over-two; one-story three-bedroom; and A-frame. Black farmers have two choices of one-story homes, though some move into two-story homes vacated by whites gone to the Halifax tract. The houses are built of plain wood-frame shiplap set on sturdy block foundations. A typical farmstead includes a house, a smokehouse, an outdoor privy, a barn, and a chicken coop. The Grants farm Units 50 and 51, sixty acres including a garden and an orchard. Their two-bedroom house initially has no electricity. "So my mother and father had a bedroom, and five children slept in one bedroom for the first few years," Gary recalls. "Our heater that winter was a brooder—that's a heater that keeps baby chicks warm."[8]

Tenants are selected for projects like Tillery through interviews and physical examinations to determine if they are reliable and healthy enough to work the land. They must be family units—a husband and wife, usually with children.

Indeed, there are many children in Tillery. So many that they fill up Tillery Chapel Rosenwald Elementary School—one of forty-six Rosenwald Schools in Halifax County and more than eight hundred in the state, built through a partnership established by Booker T. Washington, founder of the Tuskegee Institute, and Julius Rosenwald, president of Sears, Roebuck and Company, to improve rural education in Black communities.[9]

The children work the fields alongside their parents and grandparents and range outdoors, playing baseball and dodgeball, rolling tires down the dirt roads, walking on stilts made from tin cans and baling wire. "It was a wonderful place to grow up," Grant remembers. During harvest season, the kids would stay out of school two or three days a week to work the fields.

"We worked," he says. "They somehow made it fun for us." Every road in the Tillery settlement is home to dozens of children. "You were so tired when you got out of the field, but you could always go down the road to the neighbor's house and had energy enough to continue to play."

Children are also encouraged to get an education. "Growing up in a home where you were taught that you could be whatever you wanted to be, you had to achieve, and it was understood that you were going to get an education, because that was what was needed." The Tillery kids aspire to become doctors, lawyers, scientists: "Dreams of things that we had never even dreamed we could become."

When Gary accidentally demolishes a pasture fence with the family tractor, his father tells him, "Little boy, you'd better get yourself some education, or you're going to starve to death." He's not cut out for sports or mechanical work—both his brothers grow taller and stronger than him, thriving on physical activity, while he is the bookish one. He loves school, sings in the church choir, and, though he works hard at harvest time, enjoys a happy childhood.

Of the hundreds of kids who grow up in Tillery, the overwhelming majority earn their high school diplomas, and more than half go on to graduate from college. "The settlement didn't require that you go to school," Grant says. "They would have been perfectly happy for us to stay home and work and still remain ignorant. It was the parents who understood that you needed the education in order to advance."[10]

Tillery brings together a critical mass of Black families like the Grants—independent, determined, self-willed—who are property owners. The result is a community that takes charge of its own future. They demand better schools, the right to vote.

As in so many areas of civic life in Tillery, Florenza Grant again leads the way. When she attempts to register to vote, the registrar requires her to read the Constitution—an illegal literacy test. Meanwhile, a young blond white woman is signed up without any test. When Florenza objects, the registrar tells her that the white woman is covered by the "grandfather clause" because her grandfather was white. "My mother said, 'Well, my grandfather was white—give me the Constitution,' and I mean it just pissed her off to such a degree she read the Constitution to him and then that was the day that she registered." Florenza becomes the first Black woman in Tillery to register to vote.[11]

But segregation is still very much in force, and Black farmers learn to be alert to the white brokers who buy their crops at the Tillery market. "The owner-manager would—if peanuts were selling for ten-point-nine cents a pound—he would tell the Black farmer, well that point-nine is nothing, you don't need to worry

In 1938, Tillery children learned firsthand that farm life wasn't easy. Many took the lessons learned in the field, at their mother's knee, on to higher education.

about that," Grant explains. "So you think about three thousand pounds of peanuts that you lost nine-tenths of a cent per pound and how much money you lost. Once we figured that out and got the point-nine, then they put in the grading system—different for the peanuts being grown by Blacks and those grown on the farms owned by whites."[12]

One fight at a time, the Black landowners of Tillery take charge of their world, insisting on being treated fairly and with respect. They support one another, find strength in solidarity. Tillery becomes more than just a farming community: it becomes an engine of transformation.

Owning their own land gives the Black residents of Tillery a power the sharecroppers do not enjoy. Grant sees it firsthand: "The local whites saw the Blacks who came here as smart aleck quote 'n-----s' and taught the sharecroppers that you don't want to get involved with them because it only leads to trouble."[13]

When the neighboring sharecroppers work for wages on Tillery farms, Grant says, "they began to understand—and be treated like real human beings." So the Tillery effect reaches far beyond the resettlement project.

Grant witnesses the difference that land ownership makes in being treated with respect. "It was transformative, no doubt about it. The Resettles were not fearful because they were working for themselves. So the local stores could not cut their credit off. They could not put them out of their homes. Racism was still very rampant and evident, but you were working to buy your own place, and that made a difference."

There is strength in numbers. "They're not going to go away and they're not going to give up on what they know is right for them. Best way I can sum it up is, we had guns. The Klan might bother the sharecroppers, but they didn't come over into the resettlement community because—as they say—'they will shoot back.' "

All told, more than two hundred Black families eventually own farms in Tillery—a generational wealth that will be passed on to children and grandchildren. Many of the farmsteads sprout small cemeteries where the older generations remain on the land they worked—land that their descendants will own for more generations to come.

Gary Grant grows into a man of solid convictions, joins the campaign for civil rights, graduates from North Carolina College at Durham (later North Carolina Central University), then returns to Tillery to teach elementary school for more than a decade—English, speech, drama, history, and science.

"I came back, and I taught school here for eleven years and introduced kids to things that they had not had opportunity to participate in," Grant recalls. With no school bus available, he loads a class full of kids into the back of his father's half-ton pickup and rides them around the community, showing them significant landmarks and instructing them in their heritage. Each student brings along some item from home that carries a history. "And they ended up bringing the cast irons that they had never seen before, washbasins that had been sitting on the shelf and they never knew anything about it before," he remembers. "Once they were challenged, they were awakened and found out that *they* had something of value."[14]

The Tillery Farms Resettlement Project is far from a utopia—its residents continue to battle the racism so deeply embedded in the surrounding culture and the federal bureaucracy itself. But for the farming families here and the generations that follow, it is on these low-lying fields that the long-deferred dream of land ownership comes true.

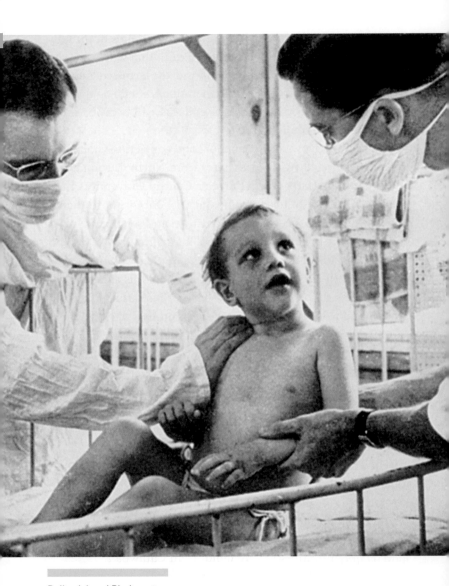

Polio claimed Piedmont
communities' most vulnerable
residents: its children.
Desperate parents seeking
a nonexistent cure went to
Hickory in search of a miracle.

CHAPTER 7

THEIR FINEST HOUR

L ike so many wartime efforts, it is conceived in emergency and executed in urgent haste, with minimal preparation, by a team of volunteers organized and led by professionals. How else to build a fully equipped emergency quarantine hospital in fifty-four hours?

The emergency strikes the home front. Even as more than 150,000 Allied troops are storming the beaches of Normandy, France, a stealthy killer is infiltrating the western Piedmont of North Carolina: polio.[1]

The first case is diagnosed in Catawba County, northwest of Charlotte, on May 30—almost a week before D-Day. Seven days after D-Day, twenty-six more children in Catawba and neighboring counties have been diagnosed with the disease. Many call it "infantile paralysis" because it usually strikes infants and very young children. Its full medical name, poliomyelitis, derives from Greek—*polios* for "gray" and *myelon* for "marrow." The poliovirus attacks the tissue at the center of the spinal cord, causing temporary weakening of the limbs, permanent paralysis (one case out of every two hundred), and when breathing muscles are paralyzed, as happens in 5 to 10 percent of cases, even death.[2]

The mysterious nature of polio instills a sense of terrifying powerlessness—in parents, city officials, even doctors. Experts know that polio is caused by a virus, but exactly how it spreads is a matter of debate: Many believe the vectors of contagion are flies. Some believe the virus is airborne. Researchers have figured out that the virus enters a victim through the nose or mouth—how, then, does it pass into the spinal column?

The *Greensboro Daily News* of August 11, 1944, enumerates all the things doctors don't know about polio, among them: "Why the disease cripples some, kills some, and the manner in which it attacks different people in entirely different ways is all still a complete and absolute mystery to medical science."[3]

Other mysteries: Why does polio strike in the summertime? Why has the age of victims steadily risen for decades, so that what was originally a malady of babies and infants now afflicts even teenagers and young adults? And why does it attack otherwise healthy children—and some adults—living in relatively clean communities? Unlike epidemics of previous eras—smallpox, typhus, cholera, diphtheria—polio does not ravage crowded urban tenements with poor sanitation, but rural and small-town communities. Middle-class, even upper-class families seem hardest hit. Polio can infect a patient for up to ten days before symptoms occur—and then they are often easy to mistake for a cold or flu: headache, fever, difficulty breathing, sore throat, vomiting, fatigue, stiff neck, aching of the limbs and back. Only a small percentage of victims initially exhibit paralysis of one or both legs. And almost three out of four show no symptoms at all—and yet are just as contagious as those who do. The virus can thrive in a community for as long as a month before anyone realizes polio has struck.[4]

When the first cases are reported in the western Piedmont, movie theaters, libraries, and swimming pools close. Shaking hands with a neighbor is considered too risky. People avoid congregating even in churches for fear of contagion. Drivers passing through affected towns roll up their windows tight despite the heat, afraid to breathe the same air that has infected polio victims. Some parents are afraid to admit that their children have polio, even to themselves—for fear of being ostracized by their neighbors. Around the country, polio victims, typically five years old and younger, are taken from their families and isolated without visitors for weeks, months.

There is no cure for polio. No medicine can reverse its pernicious effects.

Nor is there a sure way to prevent contracting it. Parents can keep a clean house, encourage the best hygiene habits in their children, feed them good food, get them regular health checkups, keep them away from crowds—do everything right—and still suffer the agony of watching their child succumb to sickness, paralysis, or death. Indeed, many doctors believe that bright, attractive children are especially vulnerable because they are more popular and therefore more socially active.

Doctors across the country try a variety of treatments—from painful surgery and immobilization of limbs in casts, to less drastic therapies now in use: Kenny massage and hot packs (named for the crusading self-trained Australian bush nurse, Sister Elizabeth Kenny), manipulation of affected limbs, compresses, and hydrotherapy. Immersion in water is championed by President Franklin D. Roosevelt, who contracted the disease at the unusual age of thirty-nine at the family getaway on Campobello Island, Canada, after a strenuous day of sailing, hiking, fighting a brushfire, and swimming in the Bay of Fundy in what he described as "water so cold it seemed paralyzing." The last photograph of Roosevelt walking unassisted is snapped at the Boy Scout jamboree at Hyde Park just before the trip, a likely ground of contagion for polio.[5]

Like many polio victims, Roosevelt—misdiagnosed by the first doctor on the scene and treated by the second in a manner that likely worsened his suffering—tries every remedy available and finally discovers the hot mineral baths at Warm Springs, Georgia. He is so heartened by his treatment there—the water buoys his spirits as well as his paralyzed legs—that he buys the place and expands it, becoming a frequent presence there and taking on the air of a wise doctor.

He uses the bully pulpit of the presidency to champion the National Foundation for Infantile Paralysis, known for its fund-raising campaign: the March of Dimes. Celebrities, including movies stars such as Ronald Reagan, Grace Kelly, and Jimmy Stewart, regularly host fundraisers. Movie houses all over the country collect dimes toward treating victims and curing the disease. The effort is wildly successful—a good thing, because it costs $1,000 per year to treat a single polio patient.[6]

Before long, both the State Orthopedic Hospital in Gastonia and Charlotte Memorial Hospital are overwhelmed with polio patients—even after both convert other wards to polio isolation wards. Dr. C. H. Crabtree of the National Foundation for Infantile Paralysis arrives on the scene to consult. The army loans him three large tents, now outfitted as polio wards on the grounds of Memorial and staffed by Red Cross nurses and a physical therapist.

The epicenter of the outbreak, Hickory, located fifty-five miles northwest of Charlotte, is the logical place for parents in outlying rural areas to bring their stricken kids—but the town of fifteen thousand has no hospital. Dr. Crabtree travels to Hickory to investigate. There he confers with Dr. A. Gaither Hahn, chairman of the Catawba County Chapter of the Foundation for Infantile Paralysis, and Dr. H. C. Whims, a dual-county health officer.

They agree that Hickory needs to open a hospital, fast. What buildings are available—any schools, churches? Dr. Hahn offers a radical proposal: commandeer Lake Hickory Health Camp, three miles outside of town. It has just one U-shaped stone building, erected by the Works Progress Administration (WPA) during the Depression. It's a "fresh air" camp on more than sixty acres of woodland where underprivileged kids can enjoy the freedom and benefits of being outdoors. Dr. Whims has authority over the facility—their plans will not have to languish as they navigate weeks of red tape and approvals. It is decided. Dr. Whims calls Mrs. Earle Townsend at the camp and directs her to send all the campers home within the hour. He organizes a convoy of cars to ferry the campers home. Then he enlists Townsend as dietician for the nascent Hickory Emergency Infantile Paralysis Hospital.

The three doctors each take on clearly defined duties: Dr. Whims supervises renovating the camp as a hospital and adding wards—first army tents, later more durable wooden structures connected by boardwalks. Dr. Hahn finds supplies and equipment. Dr. Crabtree uses his national contacts to secure funds and recruit staff from all over the United States. Within weeks, the hospital fields a remarkable cadre of doctors, nurses, and therapists from cities like Winston-Salem, Philadelphia, and Chicago and medical schools at Harvard, Yale, Johns Hopkins, and elsewhere.

Student nurses—known as "Angels of Mercy"—are recruited from nursing schools, bused in to work weekends and days off, and, like other staff, boarded in the homes of local families for free. Police officers taxi them back and forth, and regular cab drivers work without pay. The school district lends a bus.

Dr. Whims must quickly find someone who can create a blueprint for a new hospital, so he calls on a team of local architects—Mr. and Mrs. Q. E. Herman. He lays out the challenge, then hustles them into his car for the fast ride out to the camp. The Hermans sketch plans for the facility on the spot, and construction begins that same day.

Truckloads of donated lumber and other materials arrive from Herman & Sipe, Hutton & Bourbonnais, and Cline Lumber Company. When it is used up, more trucks show up with more lumber. Floodlights sprout on the building site so work can continue after dark.

Carpenters, electricians, and plumbers all lend their expertise. Lawyers, dentists, secretaries, bankers, teachers—all pitch in, fetching and carrying, hammering and painting, cleaning up debris and hauling away trash, scrubbing and cleaning the old building. Technicians from the telephone company install a new switchboard while Duke Power boosts the electricity supply. Prison work gangs hand-dig a three-mile water main conduit. The Hickory Fire Department installs hydrants. Time and again the army provides drivers and laborers, vehicles, tools, and tents. A contingent from the women's prison in Raleigh is granted temporary parole to staff the kitchen and laundry.

Radio station WHKY broadcasts a list of items the hospital needs: beds, cribs, washing machines, refrigerators, office furniture, sheets, even a can opener—and it all somehow appears on site, along with a small army of volunteers to staff the offices and comfort the victims' parents. Farmers truck in fresh fruits and vegetables. Women deliver meals they have made at home.

From his old friend Col. Frank Wilson, in charge of Moore General Hospital near Asheville, Dr. Hahn finagles fifty-five army hospital beds and mattresses. Rain dampens the efforts overnight, but the throng keeps working. In the morning the army beds arrive.

Signs go up: Arrows point to the hospital, and other signs warn that ALL VISITORS MUST RECEIVE PERMISSION TO ENTER WARD AREA.

Fifty-four hours after the architects complete their hasty sketches, the first patients are admitted to the sudden hospital. Diagnosis is made by drawing spinal fluid with a hypodermic needle—a painful procedure.[7]

And they keep arriving—in private cars and ambulances, and—when the ambulances are all taken—in hearses lent by local undertakers. Some of the kids arrive too late, likely victims of the bulbar strain of polio, which paralyzes the breathing muscles and causes suffocation. Dr. Hahn retains a bitter memory of such arrivals, as the *Hickory Daily Record* reports long after the epidemic: "It was opening the door of ambulance after ambulance one night and finding the children within them dead. One mother rose from her crouching position over her child and put a finger to her lips. 'Sh-h-h,' she whispered. 'He has been sleeping ever since we left Charlotte.' The child was dead."[8]

The public health officials make an early, crucial decision: treatment will be color-blind. The next patient—white or Black—gets the next bed. In Charlotte, Black children are relegated to a segregated basement ward where their own families must provide care. Here at Hickory, the medical and volunteer staff will care for all children, regardless of race—though as the hospital expands, Black patients are eventually segregated into their own ward.[9]

They procure iron lungs that use changes in air pressure to inflate the lungs of patients—the only treatment that can save a patient with paralyzed breathing muscles. With luck, the stricken children will progress beyond paralysis and, after a few weeks or months, escape the iron lung.

The treatment is as humane as can be managed with such a

debilitating disease: hydrotherapy, muscle massage, and gentle manipulation of afflicted limbs. Kenny hot packs are commonly applied: strips of woolen blankets boiled in water for twenty minutes, wrung dry, then wrapped around the stricken limb. The aroma of boiled wool is one that many patients will remember for a lifetime.

When no longer needed by the patient for whom they were shaped, the woolen hot packs are burned. No garbage or medical waste is allowed to leave the facility.

Health officials theorize later that the virus spread from outhouses used by those first infected, seeped into wells and rinsed into the many creeks and streams that web the Piedmont counties. Kids cooling off in their favorite swimming holes likely brought it home and into town. Ironically, the very cleanliness of their households conspired against them. In crowded tenements, enough infants would be exposed to a mild form of the virus to develop immunity—especially if still breastfeeding and sharing the mother's immunity. But as children from clean, uncrowded homes grow older with no immunity, the virus strikes more virulently.

The 1944 outbreak is not the last for North Carolina. Two years later, in summer 1948, polio strikes again—more than 2,500 cases. Guilford County suffers more cases per capita than any other county. In Greensboro, local officials take swift and prudent action. The Army Overseas Replacement Depot on Bessemer Avenue is converted to a makeshift hospital. Meanwhile, civic leaders begin a crash program of fundraising and building, and in a little over three months open the new Central Carolina Convalescent Hospital—known as the "Polio Hospital"—the second largest polio care facility in the world. Beginning with the 116 children in the depot building and another temporary facility, it takes in and treats white and Black children equally—they share wards, with white and Black nurses working side by side.

The man in charge of procurement for the hospital, John R. Foster, gets a call from a prominent politically active attorney. According to Foster, the attorney says, "John, I understand that your patients out at the hospital—that the black patients and the white patients are side by side in the units. . . . The governor called me and wanted to know about it and questioned whether or not it should be done."

Foster replies, "You go back to the governor and you tell him if he wants to be crucified politically, just bring that up as an issue."

So for the duration of the crisis—and only that long—segregation is set aside.

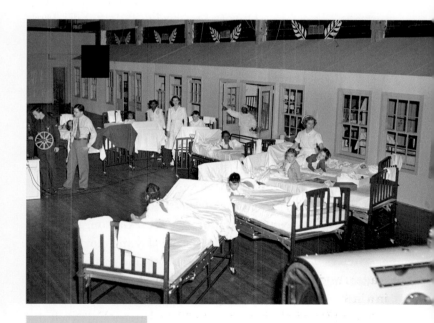

The 1944 polio outbreak is not the last for North Carolina. In 1948, the virus strikes again. In Greensboro, the Army Overseas Replacement Depot is converted to a makeshift hospital, where children are treated regardless of race.

And as at Hickory, the response of the community is overwhelming. Union men work alongside nonunion men with no animosity; restaurants donate meals seven days a week; volunteers swarm the grounds. Foster reports, "People were so anxious to do things, you almost had to look around for something to assign them."[10]

The successful public health responses in Greensboro and Hickory help drive the state to become the first to require polio vaccinations of schoolchildren.

During the next nine months of 1944–45, the staff of the Hickory Emergency Infantile Paralysis Hospital treats 454 children afflicted with polio. They do not save all of them: twelve die, and many more are paralyzed, some permanently. But the death rate is remarkably low—statistically, between twenty-two and forty-five should have died. Hickory has beaten the odds. To the March of Dimes—which brags about Hickory on its posters—and to magazines around the country, the hospital becomes "the Miracle of Hickory."

Hickory, unfortunately, has been stigmatized as "Polio City"—unfairly, because the city's infection rate is actually low but it has publicly lent its expertise and effort to helping all victims in a large radius around it.

A short film, *The Miracle at Hickory*, plays as a theatrical trailer across the country. Its narrator, Greer Garson, goes on to play Eleanor Roosevelt in both the stage play and movie *Sunrise at Campobello*—the story of FDR's paralysis and partial recovery.

But "miracle" implies a kind of magical happening, a supernatural intervention. In fact, the successful effort to save so many children comes about because of a series of brave and timely decisions made by principled men and women, then by the shared effort and sacrifice of hundreds of others. It comes about because of determination and a willingness to share resources in a time of scarcity—and out of community pride, out of an old-fashioned American spirit of can-do, and out of abundant compassion. It is precisely the opposite of waiting for divine intervention to save the day: ordinary people work together and save the day themselves. The people of Hickory turn a nightmare emergency into a memorable shared legacy.

"Polio City"—once a moniker of fear—becomes a badge of honor.[11]

On March 5, 1945, with the worst of the crisis past, Hickory transfers its remaining patients to the hospital in Charlotte.[11]

Scarcely a month later, on April 12, President Roosevelt—the secular saint of polio victims—dies of a cerebral hemorrhage at "the Little White House" in Warm Springs, Georgia. The train carrying his body back to Washington stops over in Charlotte the following evening to take on fresh flowers. The flowers that accompanied his casket thus far on its journey—including roses—are given out to the children in the polio wards of Charlotte Memorial Hospital—some in full bloom, some still in bud.[12]

Construction of the highest dam east of the Rockies began in January 1942; just three years later, Fontana Dam was generating power for the war effort.

CHAPTER

THE
GREAT FONTANA DAM

The memory endures for a lifetime: Juanita Shook, five years old, is standing beside her grandfather on his farm on the north slope of the valley of the Little Tennessee River some thirty miles west of Bryson City. It is just months after the bombing of Pearl Harbor.

A man from the Tennessee Valley Authority (TVA) comes walking toward them. He has been here before, done his best to persuade her grandfather, Scott Anthony Shook, to give up his ground. It is needed for the war effort, the man says.

By now, almost all the neighbors have left. The tenants who boarded free at the empty houses on the place have all left. The man holds out a check and says, "Now, Mister Anthony, you take this check and be out by Monday."

"Finally, at last, Grandpa reached up and took the check, and his hand was trembling," Juanita recalls. "And he folded it and put it in the bib of his overalls."

The TVA man turns and walks back to his car. What happens next imprints the memory painfully deeper: "And when he went into the house and told Grandmother about it, Grandmother cried," Juanita says. "I was little, but I mean, that broke my heart. I can remember it better than about anything, because my grandmother was my love, and I couldn't stand to see her cry."

Juanita wants to grab that check, chase down the TVA man, and give it back—and make her grandmother stop crying. But it's too late. The man is gone. The farm is gone. Once families like the Shooks have cleared out, the TVA men knock down and burn the houses and barns and outbuildings to keep people from returning. The TVA has paid on average about fifty dollars an acre for the land.[1]

The plan has been set in motion by a bill signed into law by President Roosevelt on New Year's Day, 1942. Those removed from the land are told that a new dam will flood the valley and supply power to the Alcoa aluminum plant across the mountains in Tennessee, vital for aircraft production. The real reason for the project remains a closely guarded secret, not shared with the evicted farmers: Fontana Dam will also provide power for the development of an atomic weapon in Oak Ridge, Tennessee.

Before the water can come, the people and their settlements must be gone. Low-lying cemeteries are moved out of the valley, beyond the reach of the water, but more than a thousand graves remain undisturbed on the high ground of the north shore.[2]

Thus begins the construction of the massive Fontana Dam.

The town of Fontana is founded three different times, first in 1906 as an unnamed lumber camp on Eagle Creek, a Spartan place of tents and sawmills. A few years later, it is established as a real community of wooden buildings at the confluence of Eagle Creek and the Little Tennessee—including a commissary, houses, and a hotel. The wife of the Montvale Lumber Company's vice president, Mrs. George Leidy Wood, christens the settlement "Fontana." She writes, "I thought of the lovely flowering glens, the waterfalls that looked like fountains, leaping from ledge to ledge, and eventually worked out the word 'Fontana,' a short word, musical, easy to spell."[3]

The scattered settlements around Fontana are really one community, connected by common struggles, an ethic of sharing and sacrifice, and family ties that go back many generations. Nobody is rich, but everybody seems to have enough. The farms are not the lush flat acreage of the Piedmont, but rugged, hardscrabble acres carved into the hills. The farmers harvest vegetables for the family, fruit from small orchards. Each family keeps a hog, left to roam free and gorge on windfall chestnuts all summer, before intensive logging and the blight wipe out the chestnut trees in the late 1930s. Come fall, each farmer rounds up a hog—not necessarily his own—and butchers it for the winter larder.

During the Depression, farmers find extra work on logging crews or in the copper mines. Roads are mostly graded dirt or gravel—only the main highway to Bryson City is blacktopped. Families transport themselves and their goods on horseback or in wagons or sleds drawn by horses, mules, or oxen. Few have ever traveled far beyond their home county—Swain or Graham. Settlements are named for the dominant families—"residenters"—that established them in the 1800s: Kirkland Branch, Welch Cove, Cable Cove, Murphy Branch.[4]

In 1931, after the timber is logged out, Montvale sells the town to the North Carolina Exploration Company, a copper-mining outfit. Finally, in 1942, the federal government creates a new Fontana Village in Welch Cove, above the river—about two miles from the dam-building site. The old Fontana will be drowned by the lake behind the dam—along with the wooden hotel at Bushnell, where Juanita Shook was born.

Ten miles of new road and a steel bridge are constructed to

access Fontana. Almost overnight, the TVA transforms the remote site into the second largest city in western North Carolina, home to more than five thousand workers.[5]

To attract skilled labor, scarce in wartime, the government provides housing: trailers stacked on hillsides for most, bungalows for others, a dormitory for unmarried men, and separate housing, a cafeteria, and a school for Black workers' families— even here, in the midst of a massive and urgent war effort, segregation holds fast.

Police patrol the steep graded roads on horseback.

All families have access to communal washhouses. A shopping center and cafeteria serve the new residents, and for such a large population engaged in such dangerous work, a fifty-bed hospital is built astride the road leading from Fontana to the work site. A school with nineteen classrooms accommodates some five hundred white children from forty-six states. The school auditorium doubles as a movie theater, church, and civic center.[6]

A large contingent of kids winds up sharing a vivid slice of their childhood at Fontana, while their fathers labor on the dam and their mothers tend the families, many of them also working in the offices, stores, or hospital.

One of the children, John Barton, arrives at the age of five with his two older brothers and a sister. He stays until he completes second grade. His father drives a bulldozer to clear the site for construction. "We just kind of ran wild," Barton remembers. "Everybody played outside from dusk until dark. It was safe, and my dad worked nights—we didn't see much of him at all. They worked round the clock building this thing."

It's a rough-and-tumble childhood. "For entertainment, we'd get in rock fights—throw rocks at each other," Barton recounts. "I had a sister with a tooth broke out, and a brother too, and I got a bunch of scars on my head where coal and rocks bounced off it." Other kids swing on grapevines dangling on the bluffs above the village, arcing out over rooftops and road and dive-bombing targets with rocks held between clenched knees.[7]

Jeanne Huggins's father builds frameworks to hold the poured concrete. For her, Fontana is not a childhood idyll but a trial. The family is housed in a cramped trailer: "It had propane in it that stunk like a skunk! I couldn't stand the trailer." They are latecomers to Fontana. "This was somewhere around 1945, I guess," she recalls. "Anyway, they were almost finishing the dam when I got here."

One day, her mother warns her: *Do not go to the washhouse.*

"Of course that made me absolutely want to go to the washhouse," Jeanne says. "So I went to the washhouse and went around to the back from where the showers were built in at the back of the building, and there was a tub in there, and I looked at it, and it was full of blood. I mean, *blood.* And some clothes. I went back and told my mom."

"Told you not to go up there," her mother says.

"Well, I went. I want to know what happened," Jeanne replies.

Her mother then explains what the girl saw. "The man working next to my dad—they were finishing, topping off the framework for the dam. She told me they worked with safety belts. That man's broke, and he fell from the top of that dam and was crushed. They got him out and brought him up there. And she was so . . . distraught, I guess is the word. She was washing his clothes out in that tub. And I thought, *I want to get the hell out of this place!*"[8]

Wanda Presswood is seven years old when she arrives from Ducktown, Tennessee—a small copper mining town where she was insulated from the events of the world. "I didn't know who the president was," she remembers. "I didn't know we had a war going on. We had no telephone."

Her father relocates the family—including Wanda's two sisters and a brother—to Fontana in two Ford woody station wagons. He works on one of the conveyor belts that carries six million tons of crushed rock from across the river to the dam site. The equipment is being used hard and without pause, and during frequent breakdowns, he pulls a double shift. On those nights, he sends word to his wife, who drives the kids down to the foot of the dam site to deliver his lunch.

To Wanda, the spectacle is amazing: the high concrete face lit by banks of blazing floodlights creates a magical effect. "And all you saw was these levels being built—and night was day all the time! It wasn't dark ever over there—it was the most beautiful sight!"

After the dam is completed, her mom cooks a Sunday picnic of chicken and fixings. "We'd go to the bottom of the dam, and dad could take us inside the dam then—they could go in. Tell us all about it. Then, in another week, he'd say, *Mom, can you fix some chicken? We'll go to Fontana and have a picnic.'* She'd say, *Dad, we's just up there last Sunday,'* and he'd say, *Well, we need to go back again.* He was so proud of that dam. He was. He just thought that was the greatest thing."

For Wanda, the climax of any visit to the base of the dam comes on days when the lake level is lowered for inspection of the dam and water is released through the spillway tunnels, which are lined with a foot and a half of concrete and whose ends are fitted with special outlet buckets to direct the rushing tons of water upward into a plume of spray a hundred feet high that rains down for hundreds of yards downstream. Otherwise, the force of the water would be devastating.

"I always liked to see them bring the water level of the lake down for inspection, 'cause they send that water through that tunnel and fish would fly up through that water, in the air, in that water—I mean, it was so strong! And that was a sight to see! That was a sight to see!"[9]

Fontana Dam is designed to be the highest dam east of the Rockies, rising 480 feet above the riverbed, spanning the valley for 2,365 feet. The first challenge is to excavate ten to twenty feet of overburden to reach bedrock on which the framework can be set. The war leaves steel in short supply. Thus the dam is built under a skeletal steel trestle of solid concrete poured into wooden forms—nearly three million cubic yards of the stuff, manufactured on-site in giant mixers using aggregate rock quarried out

Tennessee Valley Authority employees didn't just build Fontana Dam—they also helped pay for it. In 1943, the government recognized the TVA after 90 percent of the agency bought war bonds, raising more than $16 million toward construction.

of the mountain, then crushed and combined with river water and trainloads of cement from Tennessee.

Building the dam is dangerous work. Heavy machinery is moving night and day—bulldozers, whirley cranes, conveyor belts. Workers scramble to high work sites as the structure rises. Gravity is the enemy—tools are dropped, men fall into concrete pours or are jostled off precarious scaffolds. On one occasion, a motorized shovel careens off the brink of the rock quarry and tumbles three hundred feet down the mountainside. A worker who witnesses the accident, John Lee Patterson, describes it: "It looked like a beer can mashed up when they started salvaging it." Incredibly, the operator—who rides the machine all the way to the bottom—survives with only a broken arm.

The inherent risk of heavy construction is magnified by the sheer numbers of men and machines at work outdoors in all weather—and especially by the speed with which the crews work, which means long hours, long weeks, and chronic fatigue. During construction, 14 men are killed, another 11 are permanently disabled, and 447 others suffer serious injuries.[10]

"Everything happened so fast here—no matter what was going on, it was going on fast," Paul Banks, just a boy during the construction, recalls. "That power had to be available at a certain time to get that bomb built. And they did—they dropped the bomb on time."[11]

The secret reason behind all the urgent haste is the need to provide an immense supply of electrical power to Oak Ridge, Tennessee, across the mountains, where scientists and engineers are building the first atomic bomb.

The project manager, Fred C. Schlemmer, works hard to maintain the morale of the workers and their families. Big band music blares from loudspeakers at the work site. At the entrance to the cafeteria, a sign exhorts them Work! Or Fight! For Schlemmer, hearty food is a morale booster. By 1943, the cafeteria is turning out six thousand meals a day, along with two thousand more sack lunches. Schlemmer regularly posts progress reports—how many yards of concrete poured, what other milestones the workers have reached.[12]

Schlemmer knows the pain of sacrifice for the war effort: his eldest son and namesake is killed in action at St. Lô just weeks after D-Day at the age of twenty-two.

In the remarkable span of thirty-six months—from January 1942 until January 1945—the Fontana Dam is constructed from a bare riverbed and begins generating electricity at a rate of 202.500 kilowatts per day. As on all TVA projects, a large sign on the dam proclaims, Built for the People of the United States of America—1945.

The dam backs up water in an artificial lake twenty-nine miles long and spilling over 10,670 acres—nearly seventeen square miles.[13]

Fontana Village is dismantled in 1945 almost as quickly as it was built—portable houses sold off, equipment moved to new sites, residents scattered back across the country. After the war, it enjoys a revival as a tourist resort under a contract with Government Services, Inc.—a food service corporation whose chairman of the board is Maj. Gen. Ulysses S. Grant III.

But there is a cost to Fontana Dam, more than just $70 million spent and workers' lives lost. More than just isolated houses, barns, stores, and hotels are inundated to make way for the dam—just as it is more than a collection of individuals or even families who are removed from the land. What is drowned is a greater community of hard-working, sharing neighbors and extended family. Their spirit was worked right into the land, generations deep.

Now some of them relocate to Bryson City and other mountain towns where they have kin. Others range far from their native ground, chasing jobs or trying to find new land. When the lake is down, some of their homes and barns, strangely left undisturbed by the TVA crews, appear as ghostly apparitions beneath the clear water—eerie reminders of their absence.

Left behind too are many of the graves of their pioneering forebears on the high ground on the north shore of the new lake. With old Route 288 underwater, the abandoned cemeteries are now inaccessible by land. The government promises to build a road to carry the evicted families back to those graves, but the road is never completed. It winds northwest out of Bryson City up a long series of steep switchbacks, through a tunnel blasted out of hard rock as old as the earth—and abruptly ends, arriving exactly nowhere.

The home of Tom Wallace Howard, Ocracoke's postmaster from 1902–1941, is no match for the storm's 140 mile-per-hour winds and deadly storm surge.

CHAPTER

THE
BIG BLOW
OF '**44**

I t is the most powerful storm to strike the Outer Banks in the twentieth century, packing sustained winds so powerful—140 miles per hour—that forecasters at the U.S. Weather Bureau Office in Miami christen it simply the Great Atlantic Hurricane "to convey a proper description."

It churns onto radar screens northeast of the Windward Islands in early September, tracks north of the Greater Antilles, and bears down on the Bahamas. A weather officer aboard a U.S. Army reconnaissance plane that flies into the storm off Puerto Rico reports "turbulence so great that with the pilot and copilot both at the controls the plane could not be kept under control, and several times it was feared it would be torn apart or crash out of control." Mechanics inspecting the plane later find that 150 rivets have been sheared off one wing.[1]

America is almost three years into fighting World War II, with invading Allied armies pushing across France toward Germany. On September 12, the front page of the *Rocky Mount Evening Telegram* proclaims "2 U.S. COLUMNS RAM SIEGFRIED LINE"—and in smaller type, "Hurricane Drifts Toward U.S."[2]

The heavy deployment of men and vessels along the coast leaves it especially vulnerable. About four hundred miles southeast of Cape Lookout, the destroyer USS *Warrington* and a companion ship, the USS *Hyades*, steam into the maelstrom on the evening of September 12, crossing right into the eye of the storm. Unable to proceed against the monstrous waves, the *Warrington* heaves to while the *Hyades* sails on.

By the early hours of September 13, the storm has intensified, and the breaking waves of seawater sluice down the destroyer's main vents. "The water rushing into her vents caused a loss of electrical power which set off a chain reaction," explains Ken Adams, serving as radioman aboard USS *Edsall*, who receives the *Warrington*'s uncoded distress call. Shortly after noon, seventy-foot seas roll the *Warrington* onto its side, and the destroyer slips under the sea stern-first. Ten vessels comb the ocean for survivors, rescuing just 73 of 321 officers and crew.[3]

On shore, the *Statesville Record and Landmark* reports, "Red Cross chapters from Delaware to Maine have been placed on alert." Ahead of landfall, the damage is already beginning. "Morehead City and Beaufort have been cut off from outside communication, because telephone lines east of New Bern have gone out. Police Chief Ed Bellengia of New Bern says he is informed that inhabitants are being evacuated from Beaufort, as a storm precautionary measure."

The newspaper story continues: "Cape Hatteras, feared by seamen as one of the roughest storm areas of the world, was directly in the path of the hurricane. . . . A circle of screaming winds radiated from the storm center."[4]

United Press International reports from Beaufort the same

day: "Mother Nature warned her family of the approaching Atlantic hurricane last night in plenty of time for them to scurry for
safety to high ground. Travelers evacuating the beaches reported
the head lamps of their automobiles fell upon dozens of rabbits,
dogs, cats and other animals moving inland along the highways."[5]

The Marine Corps Air Station at Cherry Point is placed on
emergency alert and turns back two truckloads of dynamite at
New Bern. Army and navy airplanes are ferried inland. Farther
south, soldiers at Camp Davis are moved away from the Onslow
Bay beaches.

The hurricane slams into the northeastern coast of North
Carolina on September 14 and devastates a region from Core
Banks to Currituck. Portsmouth Island is temporarily drowned
by the surging waters, and a tide is reported at fourteen feet. By

The forty-two-foot mail boat *Aleta* ran aground near the Island Inn on
Ocracoke. *Aleta* carried mail and passengers between Ocracoke Island
and the town of Atlantic in Carteret County during the 1940s and '50s.

7:00 a.m. the wind is already blowing eighty-six miles per hour. Before long, it is over one hundred miles per hour.[6]

The mail boat *Aleta* runs aground near the Island Inn on Ocracoke, rammed onto the beach cheek by jowl with a fishing boat.

The streets of Ocracoke Island turn into rivers. Big Ike O'Neal, an Ocracoker, opens the front and back doors of his house to let the water rush through and keep the structure from washing away.

For the first time since it was erected in 1823, rising waters threaten the Ocracoke Lighthouse. Keeper Joe Burris reports that the waters lap at its base and flood the keeper's quarters half a foot deep before receding.[7]

A Coast Guardsman stationed there, on a call with the Portsmouth Station, tells his fellow operator he sees no surge. "And then," he records, "whilst I was talking, I looked out across the lighthouse lawn, and there she was a'comin', and before I hung up the receiver, she was around me feet."[8]

Numerous houses are damaged, and six are completely destroyed. Damage at Ocracoke is estimated at half a million dollars. The village water tank is knocked down, and the islanders are without drinking water. Fifteen evacuees make it to New Bern two days after the storm. Many, such as Mrs. William Robert Smith, report that their families have lost everything but the clothes they are wearing.[9]

The hurricane moves up the coast, striking Hatteras Island. There, fishing boats are slammed onto the shoals, damaged or sunk.

Wallace Royce Haywood, a young boy at the time, remembers the storm: "We were in a neighbor's house in Avon, on the second floor—and the water was up to my mother's knees! I saw houses floating by out the window." He later winds up on the cover of *Life* magazine, barefoot and perched on a dredge pipe, in a 1947 feature that identifies him as "the 6-year-old son, grandson, and great-grandson of Hatteras fishermen."[10]

O. G. Gray, a merchant in Avon, is worried about a stash of money and war bonds that his fellow villagers have left in his safe. "When it became apparent that everything in the little store might be lost, the merchant left his home and rushed to his store," recounts the *Burlington Daily Times-News*. "There the water was knee deep. He opened his safe and snatched up the town-folks' money and bonds and wrapped them in a bundle. He started to go home, but when he looked out the front window, he saw the turbulent tide carry away his house."

Gray's timing is bad—he's trapped inside the store as the backside of the storm spins in and the building floats away with him inside. He manages to escape with his bundle into a tree, where he hangs on for three hours. Avon has become a floating village—houses and sheds rocking past on the waves. Luckily for him, his house—his family still inside—drifts less than a mile before it grounds on sand. Others are carried into the surf. Gray later helps distribute food provided by the Red Cross.[11]

Indeed, moving the surge-scattered houses back to their original sites will prove one of the most vexing tasks the islanders face. In Avon, only twelve homes are left standing and in Rodanthe just two remain. Some three hundred families seek relief from the Red Cross.[12]

Near Salvo, the Gull Shoal Coast Guard Station is swept off its foundations and carried along the beach for a quarter of a mile before fetching up in the pounding breakers. "Africa was a picnic compared to this," Captain Willie Wescott—just returned from fighting Rommel's troops—says. "I was just plain scared." The demolished station goes permanently out of service.[13]

On Bodie Island, "L.S. Parkerson, hotel proprietor at Nags Head, was shocked unconscious Thursday by a live wire falling on his car," reports the *Statesville Record.* "He died later." He is the single civilian fatality in North Carolina.[14]

Waves breaking one hundred feet high overwhelm and sink two Coast Guard cutters—the *Bedloe* and the *Jackson.* Both go down off Oregon Inlet while escorting the torpedoed Liberty Ship *George Ade* in sight of Bodie Island Light. The Liberty Ship somehow makes it safely into port.

"Struck four times by towering waves, the *Bedloe* tossed like a matchstick in the ocean before going down," the Coast Guard reports. The entire complement of thirty-eight officers and crew abandons ship safely. "However, the strain of fighting the hurricane aboard the 125-foot cutter, plus the ordeal of hanging to life rafts for more than fifty hours, proved too much for most of the waterlogged men and only twelve were able to hang on until rescued. One man slid under the water only minutes before the rescue craft came into sight."

Of the *Jackson*, the Coast Guard details an equally grim fate: "Borne to the top of a huge swell, the ship was struck by two swells and rolled over until the mast dipped water. As the swells subsided, the ship righted and was hit by another high sea and turned on her side a second time. Struggling out of that, the vessel was carried high by a third sea. It seemed then, survivors said, that she clung in mid-air for seconds; then the wind seized her, turned her on her side and completely over. She disappeared under a huge wave." Twenty-five men, including the twenty-three-year-old skipper, Lt. (j.g.) Norman D. Call, go down with the ship.[15]

Coast Guardsmen from the Kill Devil Hills Station—descendants of the men who once helped launch the Wright brothers into history—led by Captain Midgett, spend the day rescuing stranded residents. The wind is so fierce and unrelenting that, as the day wears on, it's no longer possible to walk upright. One of the refugees inside the station, J. A. Burglass, reports that "it was necessary for them to crawl on their bellies when they went out shortly before noon."

The northwest quadrant wind is blowing so hard, it scours the paint off automobiles. In Elizabeth City, it catapults one man over the top of his car and blows most of the water out of the Pasquotank River. One of the dirigible hangars has its roof peeled off, but all but one of the airships survives in good enough shape to mount a rescue patrol for the two missing cutters.[16]

According to the *Elizabeth City Daily Advance*, "Not in its entire history has Roanoke been utterly isolated from the outer world." In Manteo, floodwaters crest at five feet above ground floor level. At Fort Raleigh, home of *The Lost Colony* theater recently visited by President Roosevelt, the tops of pine trees hundreds of years old are twisted off, leaving a swatch of jagged twenty-foot-high stumps.

The damage the hurricane did to bridges along the Outer Banks cut off communities like Manteo from the mainland in the storm's aftermath.

From Elizabeth City, the Associated Press describes the damage: "Storm tides reaching 12 inches higher than any in the history of tropical storms on Roanoke Island inundated Manteo to a depth of six feet in Thursday's storm while the wind leveled the plant of the Manteo Shipbuilding Co., engaged in war contracts for the Navy Department, according to the first authentic reports reaching here from the isolated island." Wanchese, at the southern end of the island, fares even worse, bearing the brunt of a ten-foot tidal surge that wipes out three thousand feet of causeway, along with a bridge linking it to Nags Head. North along Route 158, the bridge at Coinjock has been seriously damaged by a barge torn adrift from its tow, closing the highway. When reports reach Governor Joseph Melville Broughton that private operators are charging the outrageous sum of five dollars each way to ferry cars across the narrow Intracoastal Waterway, he decrees that until the span is restored, the state will provide free ferry service.[17]

With the water supply contaminated by the over-washing saltwater, islanders have no source of potable water. The American Red Cross provides two distillation plants that can produce a combined twenty thousand gallons of fresh water. The Associated Press files a follow-up report from Norfolk: "The coast guard cutter *Pamlico*, which since yesterday has been supplying fresh water, medicine and food to the hurricane-stricken villages of the Cape Hatteras bank, today speeded to New Bern, N.C., for additional water and foodstuffs, coast guard officials here announced. Amphibious 'ducks' are helping to bring in supplies to the villages, which have received assistance from the *Pamlico* in every emergency since the 158-foot vessel was built in 1907."[18]

The Great Atlantic Hurricane whirls north, hooking seaward at Nags Head and continuing up the coast. It drives aground the 250-foot freighter *Thomas Tracy* near Rehoboth, Delaware—the ship breaks in two, but its crew are rescued. Wind and storm surge wreck the steel pier in Atlantic City and level oceanfront homes in Asbury Park, New Jersey, then batter Long Island and coastal Massachusetts and Rhode Island, inflicting damage as far north as the Canadian Maritimes. By the time it dissipates in the cold Labrador waters of the North Atlantic, the storm has claimed nearly 400 lives—344 of them military personnel, not counting those who perished on the *Warrington, Bedloe*, and *Jackson*.

The storm leaves a wake of wreckage almost a thousand miles long—a shattered aftermath of great natural violence. On the North Carolina coast alone, 108 buildings are destroyed and 675 others seriously damaged, and property and crop loss totals $1.45 million.[19]

Despite the widespread devastation up and down the coast, little is known of it to those living inland. The Red Cross report compiled by officials who overfly the trail of flattened villages is classified for "reasons of security." Due to wartime paranoia, reports about the strength of the storm and the destruction it causes are censored, lest U-boat captains lurking offshore pick up the news and move in to take advantage of the chaos onshore.[20]

In his official report for the U.S. Weather Bureau, H. C. Sumner offers dry superlatives: "Maximum wind velocities equaled or exceeded all previous records at Hatteras, Cape Henry, Atlantic City, New York and Block Island."[21]

Ken Adams, the radioman aboard the *Edsall* who logged the final distress call of the USS *Warrington*, has a more emotional, firsthand take on the hurricane: "It is difficult, at best, to describe this event," he writes. "Anyone not involved cannot understand the severity of the storm. Anyone involved can never forget."[22]

Labor strife that boiled over in 1943 continued to linger through the mid-'40s. In 1947, workers in Winston-Salem returned to the picket line at RJR to be heard.

CHAPTER

CLOSE RANKS BEFORE STRIKING

The action is planned for Friday, June 18, 1943: A handful of Black women who work in the top-floor stemmery of R. J. Reynolds Tobacco Factory No. 65 in the heart of Winston-Salem will report for their morning shift as usual, but they won't perform any work until their grievances are heard.

They labor in a sweltering, closed room whose atmosphere is thick with tobacco dust. In teams of three, they unpack the cases of bundled tobacco, untie the bundles, then feed the tobacco onto a chain between moving blades that cut the stems from the precious bright leaf. The moving chain, the whirling blades, the speed at which they must work, and the incessant pall of oily dust all make the labor dangerous and exhausting. The women in the stemmery are exposed to the worst effects of the toxic dust, which irritates the eyes and can cause tabacosis, a cousin of coal miners' black lung.

And the company-ordered speedup since May has made the work intolerable.

The women are overworked and underpaid—earning on average just forty-six cents per hour, fifteen to twenty dollars per forty-hour week—and are treated as the lowest of the low by the white foremen, sometimes even manhandled.[1]

Theodosia Gaither Simpson, a young woman with lively eyes and a bright smile whose enrollment in the Winston-Salem Teachers College was cut short by the Great Depression, has become a quiet leader among the women. Many have turned receptive to the stealthy campaign led by organizers from the United Cannery, Agricultural, Packing, and Affiliated Workers of America-Congress of Industrial Organizations (CIO)—known simply as the Tobacco Workers Organizing Committee (TWOC).

The day before the planned work stoppage, one of Simpson's coworkers, a widow with five children, is too ill to work her machine. One of the other stemmers, Geneva McClendon, recalls what happens next: "The foreman came up and told her that if she didn't catch up, 'there was the door that the carpenter left.' She started crying because she had these children to rear and nobody working but her."

It's a constant fear: more than half the working women in the city are employed by the big tobacco firms. For Black women, one of the few remaining options is domestic service.

Theodosia shares the plan with her coworkers at Machine Number 13—one of sixty-six on the floor lined in three long rows—"When we come in here tomorrow, let's not work until we get some understanding on how these people are going to be treated." It's not a threat, not a real strike—just a request for some humane consideration.[2]

The women of the stemmery are among more than sixteen thousand workers at R. J. Reynolds (RJR), the largest tobacco manufacturing plant in the world. It covers one hundred acres in downtown Winston-Salem, not far from the courthouse and city offices—an implicit reminder of the political power the company holds in a city where it pays more than a quarter of all property taxes. More than 80 percent of RJR workers are Black—including more than four thousand seasonal workers.[3]

Somehow, the line foreman finds out about the women's plan and threatens to fire them all if they go through with it. The women meet at lunchtime, huddled in a corner of the cafeteria, and change their plan: they will stop work immediately after lunch. They recruit the men in the adjacent casing room, where the loose tobacco plants are packed, to join them.

"We was catching so much hell at Reynolds that we had to do something," McClendon, Simpson's coworker and friend, later explains. "In the first place they gave you a great big workload, more than you could do. Instead of cutting down on the boxes of work, if the foreman discovered a box not tightly packed, he would roll it back to the casing room to be repacked. If you'd tell them they put too much work on you, they'd fire you. And then they stood over you and cussed you out about doing it: 'If you can't get this work out, get your clothes and get out . . .' Everybody would cry almost every day the way they would work you and talk to you. Working conditions was so bad you needed God *and* a union." She sums up their position: "It got so we wasn't going to take it anymore; we had had it."[4]

As the whistle sounds to signal a return to work, the women turn their backs to their idle machines and confront the foreman with their demands. He is taken aback and tells them he doesn't have the authority to bargain with them.

The women don't back down—the talk goes back and forth for a few minutes, and already the dynamic has changed: Black women are speaking up to a white foreman. Things can still end well for everyone—a few concessions from the company, a few more cents per hour in wages, some consideration for sick workers, and the women will go back to their machines. Then, in walks James Pickens McCardell, thirty-eight, a fifteen-year veteran "draft boy" who hauls the boxes of tobacco into the stemmery. He, too, has been complaining of feeling sick all week—he visited the company nurse just this morning—but has come back to work anyway to avoid being replaced. He steps forward and declares, "If these women'll stand up for their rights, I'm with them!" Then he keels over onto the floor, stone dead of a cerebral hemorrhage.[5]

Pandemonium erupts—some of the workers begin shouting that the company worked the poor man to death. Two hundred women stop work, and as word spreads to the fourth floor, 198 more shut down. On the third floor, 25 women walk off the job. Leaders counsel the workers to remain at their workstations, idle, rather than to try to leave the plant, and company officials order all seventy-three gates locked so no one can enter or leave the premises.[6]

Before long, company executives converge on No. 65 from the RJR headquarters two blocks away: B. C. Johnson, superintendent of the stemmeries; Edgar Bumgardner, head of the employment office; and John Clarke Whitaker, vice president for manufacturing—a balding, fleshy, bespectacled World War I navy veteran who years ago operated the first cigarette-making machine.

"We told him we were tired of the workload, tired of the boss standing over us with a whip in his hand," McClendon later recalls. "We wanted better working conditions, and we wanted more money We wanted equal pay for equal work."

It's an astonishing moment in a southern workplace where Black workers—let alone Black women—have previously been silenced for fear of retribution. Outside the company walls, across the South, Blacks have been registering to vote in record numbers, and membership in the National Association for the Advancement of Colored People (NAACP) is surging. Now these women are speaking out openly, as equals, as workers who are valuable to the company.

Whitaker, standing on a machine, remains calm—abiding by rules he himself composed to guide the behavior of foremen in such circumstances: "Foremen should quietly, and certainly with no show of antagonism, discuss any grievance." He appeals to their patriotism, tells the strikers that the war effort depends upon their work—indeed, 20 percent of all RJR's tobacco products go to the U.S. military.[7]

Simpson later recounts her part: "I guess he thought we were going to be afraid of him. Well, at this point it didn't matter to me. I had a husband who was working, and I had no children. I figured I was going to get along." She challenges him—under the Little Steel formula, a wartime measure tying wage increases to cost of living, she says, he can give them a raise.

He is astonished. "Who told you about the Little Steel formula?" he wants to know.

"Whether you know it or not, I can read and I can think. It's been in the paper."

Whitaker promises to consult the company attorney. But it's not enough—the dam of frustration has broken. Workers complain that they can't feed their families on the wages they take home, that the pace of work is too relentless, that sick workers are treated harshly and threatened with dismissal. What could have been a reasonable conversation has turned into a battle—and Whitaker makes a tactical retreat: If the workers appoint a committee, he will meet with them. Theodosia Simpson is elected to head the committee. The union organizers, until now stymied by the power of the company, have found their opening.

That evening, strike leaders gather about fifty people at the

Union Mission Holy Church to draft formal demands. They are hosted by the Reverend Frank O'Neal, rumored to be the highest-paid Black employee at RJR. O'Neal is a trim, balding man with a fashionable pencil-line moustache, known as an eloquent speaker and a man of fierce convictions. Like other well-paid Black workers, he is under significant pressure from Whitaker to support the company against the strikers. "He thought he could use me, but he couldn't do it," O'Neal relates. "I knew how they were doing my people because during the Depression that Reynolds Tobacco Company cleared $30 million profit when the

In the early days of the strike, a negotiating committee of RJR employees—including Theodosia Simpson (bottom left), the head of the committee and the de facto leader of the women who started the labor movement; union director Philip Koritz (seated center); Moranda Smith (seated right); and others—met to discuss their demands.

people were starving, standing in bread lines and soup lines."[8]

Simpson tells the crowd, "If you'd go to them one at a time you might get fired, but if you stick together, they're not going to fire you." The new plan is more radical than the one from the day before: On Friday, *all* of RJR's workers will report for their shifts, but no one will work until their grievances are addressed. The streets and front porches fill up with workers and their families clamoring to learn news of the events at No. 65. Word spreads that tomorrow will be a day of reckoning.

The next day, Friday, Simpson is named in a front-page story about the sit-down strike in the *Winston-Salem Journal* and *Twin City Sentinal*. Meanwhile 1,600 women at No. 60 and No. 60 extension—the largest of the stemmeries—report for their shift and declare they will not work until the grievances are settled. The women request that Robert "Chick" Black represent them. Black works in a little-known division that makes cigarettes from tobacco stems cooked at high pressure in conditioning chemicals—though the company advertises that it uses nothing but leaf in its products.

Black grew up dodging rocks thrown at him by gangs of white boys and is a man with a physically impressive presence—he plays pro baseball on the side. "We would draw large crowds," he reminisces years afterward. "I was like Satchel Paige and a lot of others; we just never got the chance to play in major leagues. Not patting myself on the back, but I was considered a pretty good outfielder. Pretty good guy at the plate and I could run pretty well. That's where I got the name 'Chick.' When I started chasing the ball, the fans would yell, 'Get that ball, chicken.' "[9]

The company trusts Black, so it agrees to the stemmers' demands. Officials pressure him to persuade the women to get back to work. But, again, they have miscalculated: Black sends word to coworkers around the plant and closes down the entire factory, all five floors. He does take his own crew back to his division to finish the work in progress—the stems being treated in vats of chemicals can't be left overnight or they might spontaneously combust and burn down the whole factory.

Friday becomes a kind of holiday, with idle workers visiting back and forth between stations, and when they leave their shifts, union organizers are waiting at the gates to sign them up by the hundreds.

The strike is on—one of fifty-seven strikes in the state in 1943.[10]

Even those white workers who want to remain on the job have nothing to do—without the stemmers who start the manufacturing process, there is no product to process.

The tobacco workers mob the streets until the police convince them to hold their mass meeting at Woodland Avenue School at Eleventh Street and Cleveland Avenue. The great fear is that company-hired thugs, aided by the all-white police force—who have for years been rough with neighborhoods in East Winston-Salem, where the Black workers live, most without running water or electricity—will disrupt the meeting with violence. But the company refrains from such rash action, and the meeting proceeds peacefully.

On Saturday they bury James McCardell.

On Sunday, some ten thousand workers converge on the Woodland Avenue School grounds for another mass meeting. Black later recounts, "People were out in the streets, on the sidewalks, in parked cars, standing on top of their cars. People were in trees." By overwhelming acclamation, those present vote not to return to work without a binding agreement that no strikers will be fired—as in 1928, when RJR fired two thousand workers for trying to form a union.[11]

On Monday, the entire RJR plant is shut down. Around ten thousand workers refuse to enter the gates of RJR. A wildcat strike at neighboring Brown & Williamson Tobacco Company gathers new energy—six hundred strikers remain out. That same morning, workers at the Mengel Box Company, which supplies the tobacco industry, walk out. Black workers at Hanes Knitting Company join the strike, as do maids at the Robert E. Lee Hotel. Local Black ministers preach unionism from the pulpit and pass the collection plate for the union.

On Tuesday, Whitaker signs the agreement, and the workers vote to return to work. The negotiations are difficult, testy, and complicated, stretching over months. A vote to ratify Local 22 of the Food, Tobacco, Agricultural, and Allied Workers of America (FTA), affiliated with the CIO, as their legal bargaining representative is complicated by the challenge of a rival union, the Tobacco Workers International Union (TWIU) and the company-backed R. J. Reynolds Employees' Association, both seeking to represent the workers in the bargaining.

At last, with the intervention of the National Labor Relations Board, workers are given a ballot on December 16 and 17—and overwhelmingly vote for the FTA.

For the first time in history, workers at R. J. Reynolds have successfully formed a union.

In the end, the union wins significant gains for the workers: six unpaid legal holidays per year, promotions based on seniority, a grievance procedure adjudicated by an equal number of union and company representatives, and a host of minor quality-of-life issues—including better bathroom facilities and rain tarps to protect Black workers riding in trucks. Other issues, including wages, remain hotly contested until the Fourth Regional War Labor Board issues its ruling in October 1944: a schedule of paid vacation days, beginning with one week after a year's employment; job security and seniority for union shop stewards; and wage increases, starting with a five-cent-per-hour raise after a month's employment, from forty-five to fifty cents.[12]

The union becomes strong and active in all areas of civic life, promoting affordable housing and championing the election of the Reverend Kenneth R. Williams—a much respected community figure—as alderman. He is the first Black candidate to defeat a white rival in a southern city in the twentieth century.

But the company's hostility to the union has only gone underground, and leading citizens attack it in ways subtle and direct. The CIO launches Operation Dixie, a plan to bring thirty thousand tobacco workers into the union. Organizers like Black and Simpson recruit new members at the plant. Simpson even replaces all the buttons on her dress with union buttons—and is sent home to change. The union agitates for regular wage increases and better working conditions in a series of negotiated contracts.

The industrialists of Winston-Salem create the Citizens Emergency Committee, made up of leading white citizens and widely believed to be sponsored by RJR, to challenge the validity of many union memberships. But perhaps the union's most effective adversary is the *Winston-Salem Journal and Twin City Sentinal*, owned by Gordon Gray, a large RJR stockholder.

Chester S. Davis, who styles himself an investigative reporter, begins writing a series of "exposés" tying the union to the Communist Party. In the growing postwar concern over the Soviet Union's aggression in Eastern Europe—fanned into hysteria by J. Edgar Hoover of the FBI and some members of Congress—this charge hits home. In fact, some leaders of the union are members of the Communist Party, but it's an open question just how deep their loyalty runs to communist dogma. Mostly it seems to be a pragmatic alliance—the Communist Party is one of the few institutions that actively support workers' rights.

Meanwhile, the union's victory against the tobacco giant is trumpeted far and wide—even in the pages of the communist

Daily Worker, which has long supported the CIO. Inspired by the example at RJR, workers at the Piedmont Tobacco Leaf Company on Tenth Street strike for higher wages on July 22, 1946. Thousands of RJR workers show up to support them. The picket line is peaceful until, on August 23, a squad of fifteen policemen arrive on the scene and begin swinging billy clubs and arresting people—including a pregnant woman. Philip Koritz, the new director of Local 22, grabs an officer's club in midswing and is arrested—and along with three Black workers is sentenced to hard labor; for him, six months of breaking rocks

Inspired by the example set at RJR, workers at the Piedmont Leaf Tobacco Company went on strike for higher wages on July 22, 1946. Thousands of RJR workers showed up to support them.

on a chain gang.

In April 1947, a new strike shuts down RJR. The union demands more wage increases to reflect the plant's productivity: between 1945 and 1946, RJR's profits have increased almost 50 percent.[13]

But Davis's damaging exposés continue in the *Journal and Sentinal*, citing evidence from the House Committee on Un-American Activities—and culminating in a front-page story citing the purported confessions of leading former union officers.

The strike is settled at last on June 8, 1947—with a wage increase of twelve cents per hour. But with the stain of communist infiltration clinging to it, Local 22 is struggling. The union is under assault by the company, the government, and the newspaper, and despite its own newspaper ads rebutting Davis's exposés, mass meetings, and even a performance by singer Paul Robeson at the Woodland Avenue School, it continues to lose clout and credibility with the workers. On March 1, 1950, workers vote narrowly against allowing it to represent them any longer. Workers at R. J. Reynolds will never be effectively organized again.

Meanwhile in 1947, the state legislature, following the lead of Governor Robert Gregg Cherry, makes it illegal to enter into a contract calling for a closed union shop—effectively crippling workers' rights to unionize in North Carolina.[14]

Black Mountain College's
Studies Building, which was
built by students and faculty.

LEARNING
THE
BLACK MOUNTAIN
WAY

The setting is idyllic, chosen for its peaceful remoteness and ability to inspire. It occupies more than six hundred acres of rolling meadowland tucked into a valley of the Great Craggy Mountains, watered by a creek that drains into Lake Eden: Black Mountain College.

The whole enterprise is a dare—a bet on a very radical design for an educational institution. It is founded in 1933 by John Andrew Rice, an unconventional professor of classics who was dismissed from Rollins College in Florida on a variety of bizarre, unfounded charges—including that he walked on a beach in a jockstrap (it was gym shorts), discouraged a female student from joining a sorority (he believed they limited other friendships), and called debates "a pernicious form of public perversion" (because debaters, in his view, cared only about winning, not about finding truth).

Rice now undertakes a new kind of college, one not stifled by arcane rules, one that addresses the whole student, not just the intellect. His collaborators include Ralph Reed Lounsbury, a professor of American Government, and Frederick Raymond Georgia, a chemist—both also dismissed by Rollins—and others, both faculty and students, who resigned in solidarity. The new college will intermingle the arts, sciences, humanities, social sciences, and manual labor—including farming vegetables for the dining hall. It will be a community first and foremost, a collaboration of faculty and students.

John Andrew Rice, founder of Black Mountain College, believed in a communal approach to higher education.

Black Mountain College (BMC) takes shape first at the Blue Ridge Assembly, a Protestant retreat and conference center built into a hillside near the town of Black Mountain, just east of Asheville. For $4,500 per year, BMC leases the site, holding classes for the fall and spring terms, then vacating the property so the church can run its summer programs [1]

The main venue is Robert E. Lee Hall, a gargantuan, white-columned wooden building. It contains both living quarters and instruction space for the initial twenty-two students, in addition to a cavernous lobby, in which communal gatherings—meetings, concerts, debates, and lectures—are held.

BMC becomes famous—and somewhat notorious—for its faculty, who are among the most progressive and accomplished in their respective fields, and some of whom are also arrogant, uncompromising egoists.

Still, the faculty roster reads like a who's-who of important innovators in the arts, humanities, sciences, and design: Willem de Kooning, a Dutch-born abstract expressionist painter, and his wife, Elaine Fried de Kooning, also an abstract expressionist painter and a premier art critic; Heinrich Jalowetz, an Austrian conductor who studied with Schönberg in Vienna and emigrated ahead of the Nazis; Eric Russell Bentley, a British playwright and critic; Hazel Larsen Archer, a photography student at BMC who returns as its first full-time photography instructor; Walter Gropius, founder of the Bauhaus school of design; avant-garde composer John Cage; and R. Buckminster Fuller, the futuristic architect of the prefabricated cylindrical Dymaxion House—among dozens of full-time and visiting instructors.

While typical colleges teach classic literature, art, and music, BMC emphasizes the art of its own time. So when John Cage joins the faculty, he performs the twentieth-century music of French composer Erik Satie—antivirtuoso, fluid melodies containing subtle jokes on other musical genres. Cage prefaces his series of piano recitals with theoretical talks in which he attacks the German romantic tradition as personified by Wagner and Beethoven. He collaborates with choreographer Merce Cunningham on a program composed on the principles of rhythm and duration rather than narrative emotion, and he incorporates movements from everyday life into the dances.

While BMC is a roiling ferment of ideas about history, biology, physics, chemistry, philosophy, psychology, literature, and political science, it becomes perhaps best known for its bold pioneering work in the arts.

Professors defy convention. Anni Albers creates fine jewelry using steel washers, drain strainers, and paper clips—as well as elaborate geometric tapestries. Her husband, Josef Albers, paints gaudy geometric canvases that fool the eye with impossible angles of perspective.

Painters and sculptors explore geometric abstraction and vivid color. Designers like Fuller eschew the traditional architecture of compression—based on sturdy, load-bearing framing in steel or wood—and develop lightweight structures based on the principle of tension, the way a circus tent is held up by a web of ropes and poles.

Faculty artists show in the most prestigious avant-garde galleries in New York City: the Museum of Modern Art, the Peggy Guggenheim Art of This Century, and the Betty Parsons Gallery, among many others.[2]

There is no set curriculum—students confer with a mentor and design their own studies. There is no attendance policy, nor are there grades. Classes may contain as few as a single student, and rarely more than half a dozen. As Rice articulates in a letter to his brother-in-law, the aim is "to maintain some order, but at the same time, keep flexibility. And once you get things too definitely on paper, that vanishes."

Students matriculate into the junior division and then, when they feel ready, write a statement of achievement summarizing what they think they have learned in their chosen field of study. They then take a series of written and oral exams designed and administered with the help of outside experts from other college faculties. The exams may last for many hours, and the oral questioning is open to observation by the whole community. Passing the first exam set gains a student admission into the senior division, and passing a second set earns graduation.[3]

At Black Mountain, activities usually considered "extracurricular" become as important as the classes: hiking in the woods,

Josef Albers brought his approach to teaching with him from his time as an instructor at the famous German Bauhaus school of art. Black Mountain College's mountain setting inspired him to incorporate nature into his lessons on color theory.

Students and faculty pitched in on every aspect of Black Mountain life. Whether working on the college's farm or digging ditches on the college's Lake Eden campus, the sense of community grew stronger as the school year progressed.

having coffee with a mentor, putting on a play, cutting wood, hoeing a vegetable patch, playing tennis.

In 1937, with the Blue Ridge Assembly lease set to expire for good in 1941, the college acquires the Lake Eden site for $35,000. The original buildings at Lake Eden are the leftovers of a summer lodge and entertainment center developed in the 1920s: a round stone house, two stone cottages, four summer lodges, and a dining hall.[4]

But a larger building is needed. The college first commissions a design from Gropius and his partner, Marcel Breur, but later considers it too expensive to build and turns to A. Lawrence Kocher, formerly of the University of Virginia. He designs a clean, modern-style complex with four wings spreading out from a hexagonal central hall, two stories of wood-framed structure over a foundation story of stone.[5]

As a cost-saving measure, students and faculty provide free labor. In 1940, classes are scheduled so as to leave afternoons free for work. Community members work in teams to gather rocks, mix cement, and haul lumber. The Studies wing takes shape on the lake shore as the signature of BMC—classrooms on the first floor and faculty apartments and other specialized spaces on the second.

"The thing that holds Black Mountain together and keeps it from the phoniness I had feared is that they are building their new building with their own hands," writes May Sarton, the poet and novelist who lectures as a visitor in 1940, to her friend Rosalind Greene. "It is something hard to describe in words to watch [Erwin] Straus, the ex-German psychiatrist with a wonderful head of white hair throwing rocks to a young girl who throws them to a boy who sets them in the wall which others have prepared with a bed of cement." She herself lends a hand, feeling "more whole and ready for *thought* than I have in years"—concluding that in an ideal world every college would be rebuilt by each new class of freshmen to discourage "the intellectual slovenliness, immaturity, lack of reality, and sentimentality which the average college produces."[6]

The Studies Building is the only wing ever completed. In spring 1941, faculty and students work together to move the entire enterprise there on a flatbed trailer pulled by a tractor—pianos, looms, books, kitchen appliances, even the heating system they installed in Robert E. Lee Hall.

Theodore Dreier, a physics professor who resigned from Rollins in solidarity with Rice, raises much of the money needed to finance the move. But afterward, he has mixed emotions about it. "So much of the wonder of that original community came out of its architecture, which was a matter of pure luck almost," he recalls for an interviewer years afterward. Faculty and students shared quarters in Lee Hall but now are segregated. "Once we were at the new college, though there was a great deal of intimacy, the faculty were much more separated somehow from students than before."[7]

One faculty member who does not survive the move is Rice, whose imperious manner has made enemies among his colleagues, and who is finally ruined by a scandalous romantic affair with a student.

The unconventional ways of BMC soon attract the attention of a suspicious governmental agency: the FBI under J. Edgar Hoover.

In 1942, the FBI recruits an informant in a class taught by Paul Radin at the California Labor School. The Polish-born anthropologist is renowned as much for his work battling racial discrimination as for his monographs on Ojibwa, Blackfeet, Ottawa, and other Native American tribes. His lectures include "Racial Problems and Social Problems" and "Racism Refutation of the Race Theory of Hitler."

The informant reports that the professor favors full racial integration and is a member of the Communist Party. He was hounded out of California by the FBI and teaches at Black Mountain for various periods between 1941 and 1944.

A weekend trip to Knoxville by two female BMC students leads to charges of prostitution—they are found hitchhiking and sentenced to sixty days in the county workhouse. Radin steps up to their defense at a faculty meeting, asserting that the two young women "were victims of a bad class-conscious society." His remarks are reported to the FBI—and he is not invited back to teach at BMC.[8]

The FBI also keeps a file on R. Buckminster Fuller, who is visiting professor in 1948–1949. His file eventually grows to sixty-nine pages.

When the United States enters the war, the draft takes all but one male student—a polio survivor—from the campus. The GI Bill offers a reprieve in 1945, and Black Mountain enrolls more men. But BMC can't survive the wave of paranoia toward nonconformists that sweeps the country with the Red Scare, and its heyday is fading fast.

One essential contradiction is built into the very design of Black Mountain College: individual liberty exists always in tension with the ideal of a cooperative community. No one is forced to work on the farm, to haul coal, or cut trees for the new building, which can lead to resentment against those who don't pitch in. And a nearly continuous state of political infighting among factions of the faculty creates fissures and interferes with matters both practical and academic. The atmosphere is electric with both creative ferment and controversy.

One controversy that occupies years of debate is the decision of whether or not to enroll Black students. The students overwhelmingly support the move, but the faculty, though believing it the right thing to do, fear a backlash from the very conservative local community that might result in violence and spell the end of the college.

They advance cautiously into a compromise solution by inviting two Black artists to participate in the summer Music and Art Institutes, which are not part of the regular college curriculum: contralto Carol Brice and composer Roland Hayes. Brice performed at the inauguration of President Roosevelt in 1941 and is a rising star in opera and musical theater. Hayes, a lyric tenor, performs his own arrangements of Negro spirituals for her and the community and for two weeks regales them all with his stories. Their dual visit is the highlight of the season. Soon afterward, Sylvesta Martin, who attended the Institute, is enrolled as the first full-time Black student.

From the start, BMC is strapped for operating funds, relying on a few wealthy, progressive donors and the efforts of students and faculty. They enlarge the farm, try mining mica for the war effort. At one point, the faculty votes to limit their own salaries to ten dollars a month in order to cut costs. Despite all the hard work and sacrifice, the college is never more than a bad year or two away from dissolution.[9]

But its effect on a generation of students and faculty is transformative. "It was a total experience, as total as I would ever experience," recalls I. S. Nakata, a student from 1940 to 1943 who returns again from 1946 to 1948. "Black Mountain was first and foremost and always the people it attracted and held in its dream of a better community, a different kind of educational adventure."[10]

Alfred Kazin, already an acclaimed critic for his first book, *On Native Grounds*, when he joins the faculty at age twenty-nine, becomes legendary for his passionate teaching of authors such as Melville and Blake. He describes his students and colleagues as "idiosyncratic, crazy, wonderful in certain ways." He says, "They were exceptional people—exceptional in their vividness."[11]

During its sublime and turbulent existence, Black Mountain College serves nearly 1,200 students, graduating only fifty-five with formal degrees. It survives just twenty-three years—an unlikely comet shooting across the educational firmament—and the afterglow of its fiery tail endures in memory, in art, and in legend.[12]

The Marine Corps needed a place to practice amphibious landings—somewhere that could replicate the challenging beachheads they would be asked to take during the war. The Corps found what it was looking for on Onslow Beach.

CHAPTER 12

THE
DEVIL DOGS
FIND A **HOME**

They come for the beaches. As war tensions ratchet up in summer 1940, the Marine Corps needs a training ground on the East Coast—big enough to accommodate a sizable force, isolated enough to practice maneuvers and live firing of heavy weapons, and, above all, with extensive beaches on which to perfect the dangerous mission of amphibious assault.

The Commandant of the Marines, Maj. Gen. Thomas Holcomb, selects Maj. John C. McQueen to find that site—somewhere. McQueen is an Annapolis graduate and veteran of service in Haiti and Nicaragua, as well as aboard two cruisers, USS *Cleveland* and USS *Quincy*. Holcomb tells McQueen to "select a pilot . . . get a plane . . . and find us a training center." He chooses Capt. Verne McCaul, a fifteen-year veteran of the Corps.

Their aerial reconnaissance takes them from Norfolk, Virginia, clear down the Atlantic Seaboard and along the Gulf Coast as far as Corpus Christi, Texas. At Onslow Bay on the New River, they survey fourteen miles of undeveloped beaches and a large expanse of coastal pine forest and swampy wetlands not far from the Marine Corps Air Station at Cherry Point. It is difficult ground for maneuvers. Marines must train in tangled thickets, wade through mucky swamps, and contend with mosquitoes, bears, alligators, and every species of poisonous snake in North America. It turns out to be the perfect proving ground for both amphibious assault and jungle fighting.[1]

The new base encompasses 174 square miles—and it is not quite as empty as it seems from the air. Just as farmers are removed from the Little Tennessee Valley to make way for the Fontana Dam and lake and from the countryside around Fayetteville to form Fort Bragg, some 2,400 people are displaced to make way for the marines.

By April 1941, construction gets underway—eight thousand civilian workers laboring in the humid heat to build what is first called simply Marine Barracks New River. The base commander, Lt. Col. W. P. T. Hill, sets up headquarters at the Gurganus farmhouse, a two-story clapboard structure. A tobacco barn serves as a warehouse. An advance detail from the First Marine Regiment settles into a hotel and cottages on Paradise Point.

In less than two months, workers lay eight miles of railroad tracks to connect the base with the Atlantic Coast Line in Jacksonville. Equipment, supplies, and construction materials now flow into the base—and soon combat-ready marines will ship out for war on trains bound for Wilmington and other ports of embarkation on the West Coast. In September, the First Marine Division under Brig. Gen. Philip H. Torrey moves into a tent camp.[2]

The base takes shape in four phases: First, the tent camp is laid out and the naval hospital at Hadnot Point built, along with the Division Training Area and other essential facilities.

In phase two, engineers dredge channels in the New River and add piers, roads, and athletic and recreational facilities. In phase three, barracks are added for the Montford Point Marines and the Women's Reserves. By the end of phase four—which continues the addition of buildings and the expansion of training grounds—the base can accommodate more than forty thousand marines.

From the start, New River is used for advanced infantry training for marines who have completed seven weeks of rigorous basic training at Parris Island, South Carolina, or San Diego. By 1942, engineering and field medical schools are on site.[3]

Alone among all marine bases, it provides training for Marine Corps Women Reserves (MCWR)—nearly nineteen thousand of them during the course of the war. They arrive in Wilmington as civilians, five hundred at a time on troop trains. There they ride the Atlantic Coast Line to New River, where buses carry them to spartan brick barracks. They sleep on rows of bunks in open "squad bays" and use communal showers, then are roused at 0545 reveille for an intensive training program of close-order drill, physical conditioning, classroom instruction, and demonstrations of gunnery, hand-to-hand combat, heavy weapons, and landing craft. Specialist schools train the women as radio operators, drivers, mechanics, clerks, and quartermasters. Initially, some of the male drill instructors deride them as "BAMs"—"broad-assed marines." But soon the women's determination and competence win the instructors' respect.[4]

New River joins Fort Bragg and Camp Mackall (airborne troops), Marine Corps Air Station Cherry Point (fighter pilots), Camp Davis (antiaircraft artillery crews), Seymour Johnson Field (bomber crews), Laurinburg-Maxton Army Air Base (transport and glider pilots), Camp Butner (infantry), Camp Sutton (combat engineers)—altogether more than one hundred military installations representing all branches of the service.

North Carolina earns the distinction of training more troops for war than any other state in the Union.[5]

For more than a century and a half after its founding in 1775, the U.S. Marine Corps' mission was to provide security aboard navy ships, to seize and defend advanced naval stations, and to fight as an agile expeditionary force in hotspots around the world: China, Nicaragua, Haiti, the Mediterranean, the Philippines.[6]

In the Great War, marines fought in several massive pitched battles, most famously at Belleau Wood. There they stopped the German advance thirty miles short of Paris at a cost of almost ten thousand casualties—more than the corps had suffered in its entire history to that point. The French so admired their stubborn gallantry in battle that they renamed the bloody ground "Bois de la Brigade de *Marine*." The defeated Germans called them *teufel hunden*—Devil Dogs, a name that stuck.

By the 1920s, war planners focus the marines' mission on the far-flung island stations in the Pacific—naval fueling depots and later airfields that would become crucial in any campaign against the Japanese. And with this new focus comes another: amphibious assault.

The problem of getting troops ashore alive and in fighting shape in the face of a fortified enemy has long proved a conundrum. At Gallipoli in the Dardanelles in 1915, Australian and New Zealand troops attempting to land were slaughtered in the face of Turkish guns. Even in the landing at Daiquirí during the Cuban campaign of 1898, facing no resistance ashore, many American troops and horses drowned simply trying to get to the landing quays.

This is the problem that a few visionary marines set out to solve—led by Lt. Gen. John Archer Lejeune, commandant of the Marine Corps during the crucial interwar period between 1920 and 1929—as lessons learned in the Great War combine with new technology and the emerging role of aviators. Ships can fight with their multiple-caliber guns. Marines ashore can maneuver and fight using all the weapons in their arsenal. But marines in transit from ship to shore are vulnerable to long-range fire, artillery, underwater mines, and aerial attack—all from an enemy they cannot readily fight. The mission is to get as many of them ashore as quickly as possible—alive and well-equipped—to join the battle.

General Lejeune now defines the marines first and foremost as an amphibious force. With a cadre of like-minded officers, he sets about testing landing craft and devising methods by which marines work in conjunction with naval beach parties in charge of the landing boats, coordinating their assaults with covering fire from naval ships stationed offshore to soften up the landing zone. Once on the beach, marine shore parties take over to unload supplies from landing craft and move them off the beach, round up stragglers, and secure prisoners.[7]

The tactics are not perfect—assaulting marines are still at the mercy of weather and tides, unseen underwater obstructions such as coral reefs, errors in planning—and, always, enemy fire.

In November 1942, General Lejeune dies—and a month later the base is named in his honor: Marine Barracks Camp Lejeune. For some years, there is debate about how to pronounce the name correctly. In 1950, Eugenia D. Lejeune, daughter of the late General Lejeune and herself a veteran of the Marine Corp Women's Reserve, settles the matter: she explains to a local newspaper, the name is not pronounced "Le June" but "Lerzhern."[8]

By the time Pearl Harbor is attacked, inspiring eighteen thousand new recruits—though just one in five of the men who volunteer make the grade—the active-duty corps numbers some sixty-six thousand marines—all white. By war's end, it will include ten times that number. The much larger army maintains segregated units for Black soldiers and the navy restricts the duty of Black sailors to the mess hall, but the marines do not enlist them at all. General Holcomb maintains the rigid policy, commenting that "Negroes' " desire to enlist in the navy or Marine Corps "is largely, I think to break into a club that doesn't want them." Citing what he predicts will be "a definite loss of efficiency in the Marine Corps if we have to take Negroes," he tells the General Board of the Navy, "If it were a question of having a Marine Corps of 5,000 whites or 250,000 Negroes, I would rather have the whites."

But in the face of early Japanese victories in the Pacific, every branch of the service needs more men. In February 1942, the General Board of the Navy directs General Holcomb to determine which assignments could be carried out by Black marines. Holcomb accepts the new order, saying, "If it is forced upon us we must make it a success." In April 1942, President Roosevelt directs Secretary of the Navy W. Frank Knox—a veteran of the Rough Riders who fought alongside valiant Black infantry during the assault on the San Juan Heights in the Spanish-American War—to enlist Blacks in every branch of the naval service.

Headquarters first responds with a secret memo recommending that the Corps should form an all-Black raider battalion to join the other two raider battalions already in the field, "ideal for night raids as no camouflage of faces or hands would be necessary"—an idea that is quickly abandoned.

Instead, under pressure from the General Board, headquarters organizes the Fifty-first Defense Battalion (Composite) of infantry, coastal artillery, antiaircraft, armored, and maintenance personnel. By summer, nine hundred Black marines, aged seventeen to twenty-nine, from California to the Carolinas, are recruited for training at a segregated facility attached to New River Barracks—on a peninsula jutting into the New River called Montford Point.[9]

There they complete basic training, then learn marksmanship, gunnery with heavy weapons, how to deploy and operate tanks and artillery, and a variety of other supporting skills. As a defense battalion, the Fifty-first will be expected to operate independently, holding remote island airfields against Japanese attack, and its mission requires that it be self-contained and flexible, able to cover any contingency of assault from the air, land, or sea. Specialist support units—such as ammunition companies—can also expect to serve attached to assault forces.

Their officers are all white, as are their drill instructors (DI). But by 1943, Black DIs rise from the ranks and take charge of training from now on. "We thought that would be good, but we found that worse than having the white DIs, 'cause they, the blacks, were determined to make us succeed and to be real

Marines from Montford Point

Marines," recalls Joseph Carpenter, an early recruit who eventually attains the rank of lieutenant colonel. "And that was their main goal, was to be sure that we were gonna be better than everybody else."[10]

Soon they are joined by a second battalion, the Fifty-second, and by early 1944, both units find themselves deployed to the Pacific Theater.

The First Marine Division ships out in the summer of 1942 for combat on Guadalcanal, Peleliu, and Okinawa—three of the fiercest battles of the war. At Peleliu alone, in six weeks of sustained combat, more than 1,200 marines are killed in action—including men from two companies of Montford Point marines from the Fifty-first. After the war, the First Division moves to Camp Pendleton, California.

One of the Montford Point marines, Lee Douglas Jr., from Columbia, South Carolina, lands at Peleliu as part of the Seventh Ammunition Company charged with bringing ammunition ashore for the main assault troops. "You may be a mechanic. You may be a cook. But the rifle comes first . . . your second job, that's all it becomes, second," he explains. "My company, when we went in, we went with our rifles blazing. There is no secondhand nothing."

The Fifty-first deploys first to the Ellice Islands and then farther north to the Marshall Islands, to guard airfields and staging bases. Two companies of the Fifty-first hit the beach at Iwo Jima with the first assault waves and are pinned down for hours under withering fire before advancing inland. The Fifty-second participates in the last fighting on Guam, where it remains until the Japanese surrender.

More than two thousand Montford Point marines take part in the Battle of Okinawa, just four hundred miles south of the Japanese home islands. After the surrender, nine companies of

Black marines deploy to Sasebo naval base, just south of Nagasaki, to help clear the monumental scorched wreckage left in the wake of the second atomic bomb. Soon afterward, the companies of the Fifty-first and Fifty-second are disbanded one by one until, by 1947, the last are gone. A year later, President Harry Truman orders the services desegregated. In 1949, Montford Point is decommissioned. From now on, Black recruits will train at Parris Island or San Diego, with whites.[11]

The Women's Reserves deploy to bases at home and abroad, playing vital roles in quartermaster depots, offices, and repair shops—and running motor pools at Pearl Harbor and other installations, freeing male marines for combat duty.

The Second Marine Division, also trained at Camp Lejeune, fights on Guadalcanal, Tarawa, Tinian, and Okinawa—all crucial, savage battles to seize airfields for the eventual assault on Japan. The division's deadliest battle is the fight for Saipan, in which it suffers more than 6,500 casualties. Three marines from the Second are posthumously awarded the Medal of Honor for heroic conduct. The Second Division joins the occupation forces in Japan for a short stint before returning home. From now on, its permanent base will be Camp Lejeune.

The base becomes an anchor for the Jacksonville community, a key part of its identity, and unlike many other installations established in the haste of wartime exigency and just as hastily decommissioned, Camp Lejeune endures as the "Home of Expeditionary Forces in Readiness."

Governor Joseph
Melville Broughton

CHAPTER

A **MAN** FOR **HIS TIME**

Joseph Melville Broughton is a former principal of Bunn High School in Franklin County, and he looks the part, with his wire-rimmed glasses and dark hair neatly parted above a plain, often thoughtful countenance. In public photographs—shaking hands with Boy Scouts, eating ice cream at Central Piedmont Junior High School, christening a battleship—he rarely smiles. Rather, he radiates a calm gravitas appropriate for a trusted man in charge. Yet colleagues and friends are impressed with his sense of humor and talent for storytelling. He worked briefly as a newspaper reporter in Winston-Salem and now is a successful farm owner and Harvard-trained attorney living near Raleigh. In his habitual dark double-breasted suit and tie, he would not stand out in any crowd of businessmen or church elders.

Among numerous civic posts, he has served on the Raleigh School Board and as president of the Raleigh Chamber of

Commerce, the Wake County Bar Association, and the state bar association; was elected to two terms in the state senate representing Wake County—where his first act was to successfully champion a bill instituting a secret or "Australian" ballot; and served as the Protestant chairman of the North Carolina Conference of Christians and Jews. His résumé includes seats on the boards of trustees of Shaw University, the University of North Carolina, and his alma mater, Wake Forest College, where he played varsity football.

He's been married for twenty-five years to Alice Harper Willson, and they have four children: Alice Willson, Joseph Melville Jr., Robert Bain, and Woodson Harris.

Those who know him best understand him to be exactly what he appears to be: a hardworking, deeply religious man trying to make the world—and his home state—a better place. Political rivals may oppose his policies, but no one questions his integrity. He does harbor one lifelong ambition: to become a United States senator. But first there are important things to accomplish in the statehouse.

Joseph Melville Broughton is a man of his time, and the arc of his career reaches its zenith at exactly the moment when his state needs him most. In the contentious gubernatorial election of 1940, after besting six opponents in the primary, he campaigns enthusiastically for a Democratic ticket headed by President Franklin D. Roosevelt, who seeks an unprecedented third term in office. Some political observers don't like Broughton's chances—there is much popular sentiment against a presidential third term, and many predict that issue may sabotage state Democratic candidates. Instead, Roosevelt wins a healthy majority and returns to the White House.

Broughton stuns his critics: he receives the greatest number of votes ever cast for a governor in the history of the state thus far—winning by an unheard-of margin of more than fifty percentage points.[1]

That same year, Furnifold M. Simmons—the architect of white supremacy politics of the state Democratic Party at the turn of the twentieth century—dies at the age of eighty-six. It is a changing of the guard in a profound sense.

The *Journal-Patriot* of Wilkesboro reports on Broughton's swearing-in on January 9, 1941: "The new chief executive, a red carnation in the buttonhole of his morning coat, took his oath of office before more than 4,000 persons who filled every available inch of floor space in Raleigh's Memorial Auditorium."

In a decade infatuated with Hollywood glamour, Broughton would not be cast as a dashing leading man—he is instead sensible, steady, and reliable. Whenever he finds himself in the limelight of newspaper or radio coverage, it is invariably to promote a policy or serve some constituency—never to advance his own celebrity. The red carnation in his lapel, far from flamboyant, merely accentuates his otherwise sober, earnest appearance. He is neither egotistical nor vain. Indeed, his whole career has been built according to a guiding ethic—not of personal aggrandizement, but of public service.

Broughton has arrived at this moment in the unusual position of being unbound by strict campaign promises, aside from declaring he will repeal the unpopular sales tax on food for home consumption and generally support business and agriculture. In the interim between the primary and the election, the *Waynesville Mountaineer* has weighed in on this peculiar freedom: "J. Melville Broughton, North Carolina's next governor in the absence of death or a political miracle, will take office next January with very few definite commitments, either from his own or the Democratic party's platform, to tie his hands."[2]

Thus, in his inaugural address, Broughton articulates a philosophy of governance free of partisan favor: "Government in a democracy exercises its true and noblest function when it seeks to promote the welfare of all the people. . . . I shall endeavor to deal fairly, justly, and honorably with all, regardless of race, influence, or party affiliation."

With war threatening, which will likely require every resource the state can muster, another governor might elect to retrench, maintain the status quo rather than embark on ambitious programs to move the state forward. But Broughton declares a slate of progressive priorities, and at the top of his list is education: "Supreme in importance among all our state activities and agendas are the public schools." He proposes an "adequate and fair teacher retirement bill," coupled with a similar plan for other state employees; safeguards to ensure that teachers are protected from "arbitrary, capricious, or political dismissal from service"; increased salaries for teachers; a nine-month term for all public schools and the addition of twelfth grade to high schools; and more money directed toward vocational training and adult education.[3]

After a rousing ovation, the new governor proceeds outdoors to the reviewing stand to watch his own inaugural parade, kicked off by a nineteen-gun salute. "The nation's preparedness program was apparent in the complexion of the parade as wave after wave of khaki-clad troops—some on foot, some riding with big guns and new mechanized equipment from Fort Bragg—passed the stand. R.O.T.C. units, high school bands, and a coast guard squad were in the line of march," records the *Journal-Patriot*. "A squadron of bombing observation planes and a blimp flew overhead."

Spectators number 125,000—the largest inaugural crowd in memory.[4]

In office, Governor Broughton proves to be a tireless workhorse, not a show horse—the strong, calm center amid the frenzy of war preparations: the influx of hundreds of thousands of military personnel, increased agricultural and industrial production, fast-track construction of military bases, road- and dam-building, and mobilization of thousands of citizen-soldiers into a state guard. He excels at the tedious, exacting work of creating detailed policy. Though not a spellbinding orator, he speaks clearly from firm convictions and persuades the legislature to turn his policies into law.

In addition to all the duties of executive governance and wrangling the legislature, he travels extensively throughout the state, giving hundreds of speeches and meeting scores of citizens' groups at every kind of event: the Ruritan, Lions, and Kiwanis clubs in Hoke County; the Cleveland 4-H Club in Johnston County; the statewide teachers convention; the Institute of Government at the University of North Carolina at Chapel Hill; the 1941 graduating class of the North Carolina College for Negroes; the Diamond Jubilee celebration of White Rock Baptist Church in Durham; the National Wrestling and Boxing Association Conference in Winston-Salem; the launching of the first Liberty Ship, *Zebulon B. Vance*, in Wilmington. He even detonates four hundred sticks of dynamite in a ceremonial reopening of the state-owned lime mine near Limerock. The press reports that the blast echoes off Pilot Mountain, and rocky debris is catapulted into the Yadkin River. Broughton now offers farmers soil-enhancing lime at $1.25 per ton—about half of what they have been paying.[5]

He issues sixty-eight proclamations to promote morale—a rate of one every three weeks during his tenure of office: declaring Thanksgiving a holiday to be celebrated with the Stars and Stripes and the Bible; announcing the rollout of Selective Service; enlisting the aid of timber growers in the war effort; pronouncing November 10, 1942, as Marine Corps Day and October 27, 1944, as Navy Day; and in 1942 declaring the Fourth of July to be "Victory Day" with a goal of celebrations in all one hundred counties.

His wife, Alice Harper, and his daughter, Alice, do their part for the war effort—in 1943, they are photographed in the ballroom of the governor's mansion for *Vogue*, wearing "outstanding cotton creations" in support of the state's cotton textile industry.[6]

Broughton's greatest achievements are legislative—his Democratic Party controls the General Assembly—and undeniably progressive. In the realm of education, he does exactly as he promised: extends the high school curriculum through the twelfth grade, lengthens the school calendar to a full nine months, institutes a retirement plan for teachers—shared by other state employees—and wins for them a salary increase. Culturally, he leads the effort to fund libraries and museums. For the general welfare, he institutes the state's first program of workmen's compensation, expands medical care, and launches a program of hospital construction. A longtime farm owner himself, he extends state aid to farmers. In support of the war effort, he institutes a Civilian Defense program. And in keeping with his other campaign promise, he rescinds the tax on food for home consumption.[7]

He supports the efforts of Black educators and, though he doesn't support full desegregation, works to ensure equality of funding. Addressing the ninety-six graduates of the North Carolina College for Negroes in 1941, he declares, "I am glad to live in and be governor of a state that does not have to apologize for the opportunities for development and training provided for its Negro citizens. . . . In education we have not had to wait for a mandamus of court to bring equity and to give Negro boys and girls a chance for growth and progress." He exhorts them to enter skilled professions: "Let us not become educated away from usefulness"—yet also urges them to find a place in their lives for poetry and art.[8]

Limited by state law to a single term in the governor's mansion, Broughton leaves office at the height of his popularity and success. At the 1944 Democratic Convention, he is named a favorite son candidate for vice president of the United States—more an honorary nomination than a realistic one.

On December 30, in a farewell radio address to the people of the state, he matter-of-factly sums up his remarkable record of the past four years: "I make no boastful claims, and freely admit my mistakes," he tells them. "With God's help and the wholehearted cooperation of the citizens of the state, I have tried earnestly to do my best. I shall leave the high office with a heart full of love for North Carolina and for the people of the state."[9]

In June 1947, Governor Broughton addressed the crowd at the Singing on the Mountain gospel festival on Grandfather Mountain. At the time, Broughton was beginning his senatorial campaign.

Then comes an unexpected opportunity: Senator Josiah Bailey is taken ill and dies of a cerebral hemorrhage in December 1946, leaving the unexpired remainder of his term.[10] Governor R. Gregg Cherry appoints William B. Umstead, his former campaign manager, to the seat, but Broughton challenges him in the primary of 1948. His Macon County supporters run a typical ad: "A Distinguished Record of Leadership Speaks for itself to the Farmers of North Carolina." Broughton carries the primary by nearly five percentage points and wins the general election. But the crowning achievement of his political career is fated to be short-lived.

On March 7, 1949, the *Daily Tar Heel*, the campus newspaper of the University of North Carolina at Chapel Hill, reports: "The body of J. Melville Broughton came home for the last time at 7:10 o'clock this morning. The 60-year-old North Carolina Senator and former Governor died suddenly of a heart attack yesterday, only three months after he reached his life-long goal of election to the United States Senate. Today he was to have made his first speech on the senate floor, in the Southern filibuster fight. Instead he was coming home to the city where he headed North Carolina's government through four critical war years and maintained his law offices for more than a quarter of a century."[11]

At last, the energetic governor lies tranquilly in state. His funeral is held at the Tabernacle Baptist Church, where he was well known for his many years spent teaching Sunday school.

Broughton's old friend, Dr. Frank Graham, UNC's president, laments, "America has lost a leader on the very threshold of high promise and dedication to his country at a critical time."

To the astonishment of most political observers, Governor Kerr Scott appoints Graham—a well-known progressive who favors school desegregation—to fill the remainder of Broughton's term. As the *Salemite* of Salem College explains, "Although Dr.

Graham is highly esteemed by many, there are some people who regard him not as merely a liberal but as a Communist."[12]

But whatever his political views, Graham, like Broughton, is widely respected for his unassailable integrity. When pressed whether he vetted Graham prior to the appointment, Cherry responds plainly, "I didn't ask him what his stand was going to be on civil rights or any issues. I didn't ask him anything about what he'd do except become senator."[13]

It's the kind of answer Broughton himself—who always answered to conscience before all—would have approved.

CODA

The glamor has matured into substance. The grinding poverty of the Great Depression is banished for good. The war has been won. Across the great rural hinterland between cities, the darkness now is spangled with a scattered constellation of new electric lights.

ACKNOWLEDGMENTS

I am indebted to Elizabeth Hudson (Editor in Chief), Todd Dulaney (Executive Editor), Bernard Mann (President and Publisher), Katie Saintsing (Associate Editor), Katie King (Editorial Assistant), and Jason Chenier (Art Director) at *Our State* for their important roles in imagining the original *Decades* series and making it a reality. I am extremely grateful also to Lynn York and Robin Miura at Blair, whose enthusiasm and hard work shaped the book project into something special and lasting. And none of the stories in this volume would be possible without the tireless support and assistance of my wife, Jill Gerard, who accompanied me on many of my adventures into the colorful and eventful 1940s.

Others who made valuable contributions include the following:

Paul Banks of the "Fontana Dam Kids"

Bill Barker, Archivist, The Mariners' Museum and Park, Newport News, Va.

John Barton of the "Fontana Dam Kids"

Rebecca A. Baugnon, Library Specialist at William Madison Randall Library Special Collections, University of North Carolina Wilmington

Samantha Crisp, Director, Outer Banks History Center, Manteo, N.C.

Julia Ellis, fact-checker for *Our State* magazine

Ann Freeman, Wilmington

William Freeman, Wilmington

Gary R. Grant, Executive Director, Concerned Citizens of Tillery

Joseph M. Herbert, Colorado State University Center for the Environmental Management of Military Lands Research Archaeologist, Fort Bragg

Capt. Wilbur D. Jones Jr., USN retired

Earl Kirkland, Swain County Heritage Center, Bryson City, N.C.

Juanita Lester, Bryson City, N.C.

Thomas D. McCollum, Fort Bragg Garrison Public Affairs Officer and twenty-four-year veteran of the 82nd Airborne

Dwight Morrow of the "Fontana Dam Kids"

Wanda Presswood Newman of the "Fontana Dam Kids"

Cliff Pyron, North Carolina State Ports

Jeannie Huggins Revis, of the "Fontana Dam Kids"

Mary Ellen Riddle, Education Curator, Graveyard of the Atlantic Museum, Hatteras Island, N.C.

Don Stutts, writer

Rebecca Taylor, Manager, Federal Point History Center, Carolina Beach, N.C.

Nancy Wright, General William C. Lee Airborne Museum, Dunn, N.C.

PHOTOGRAPHY CREDITS

COVER

Left. Chief Standing Deer, photo by John Hemmer, NCDCR State Archives

Center. Portrait of Ava Gardner by Bert Pfeiffer, courtesy of the Ava Gardner Trust

Right. Earl Scruggs, courtesy of the Jim Mills Collection

CHAPTER 1

Page 10. Courtesy of New Hanover County Public Library

Page 15. Courtesy of New Hanover County Public Library

Page 17. Courtesy of New Hanover County Public Library

CHAPTER 2

Page 22. Courtesy of Pictorial Press Ltd./Alamy Photo

Page 27. Courtesy of Jim Mills

Page 28. William P. Gottlieb/Ira and Leonore S. Gershwin Fund Collection, Music Division, Library of Congress

Page 31. Courtesy of Wolfgang Kunz/Ullstein Bild via Getty Images

CHAPTER 3

Page 34. Courtesy of Bettmann/Getty Images

Page 38. Photo by Andrew Craft, courtesy of Imagn/*USA Today*

CHAPTER 4

Page 44. Courtesy of the North Carolina Collection, Wilson Library, University of North Carolina at Chapel Hill

Page 51. Courtesy of Hunter Library, Western Carolina University

CHAPTER 5

Page 54. Courtesy of the State Archives of North Carolina

Page 58 (both photos). Courtesy of the National Park Service, Blue Ridge Parkway Archives

Page 61. Courtesy of the State Archives of North Carolina

CHAPTER 6

Page 66. Courtesy of the Library of Congress

Page 68. Photo by Lissa Gotwals

Page 73. Courtesy of the Library of Congress

CHAPTER 7

Page 76. Courtesy of the North Carolina Museum of History, originally published in 1940 by the March of Dimes

Page 85. Courtesy of Carol W. Martin/Greensboro History Museum Collection

CHAPTER 8

Page 88. Courtesy of the Tennessee Valley Authority

Page 95. Courtesy of the Tennessee Valley Authority

CHAPTER 9

Page 100. Courtesy of Ocracoke Preservation Society

Page 103. Courtesy of Ocracoke Preservation Society

Page 107. Courtesy of the North Carolina Museum of History

CHAPTER 10

Page 110. Courtesy of the *Winston-Salem Journal*

Page 116. Courtesy of Richard Koritz

Page 121. Courtesy of Richard Koritz

CHAPTER 11

Page 124. Courtesy of the Western Regional Archives, State Archives of North Carolina

Page 126. Courtesy of the Western Regional Archives, State Archives of North Carolina

Page 129. Photo by Genevieve Naylor via Corbis/Getty Images

Page 130, top. Courtesy of the Western Regional Archives, State Archives of North Carolina

Page 130, bottom. Courtesy of Black Mountain College Museum + Arts Center

CHAPTER 12

Page 136. Courtesy of the National Archives

Page 143. Courtesy of the Department of Defense, U.S. Marine Corps

CHAPTER 13

Page 146. Courtesy of the North Carolina Museum of History

Page 153. Photo by Hugh Morton Photographs and Films, North Carolina Collection, Wilson Library, University of North Carolina at Chapel Hill

NOTES

CHAPTER 1

1. Wilbur D. Jones Jr., "Remembering the Reuben James and Its Link to Wilmington," *Wilmington Star News*, Oct. 31, 2012 (https://www.starnewsonline.com/article/NC/20121031/Opinion/605049954/WM); and the original story, Nov. 1941.

2. Mark St. John Erickson, "Shipbuilding Boss Homer L. Ferguson Shaped Yard and Region."

3. Thirty-seven Liberty ships cited in North Carolina Shipbuilding Company, *Five Years of North Carolina Shipbuilding*, 9; also number of ships and cost of $42 million in paid story, "Ship Ahoy! Wilmington Goes Ahead," in Nov. 9, 1941, edition of *Wilmington Morning Star*. The plan was conceived by agreement with the U.S. Maritime Commission based on what the yard could build in that time. Ferguson approved the new site in Wilmington so as not to compete with the Newport News site.

4. Initially 56.9 acres with 27 additional acres added fairly quickly. The yard kept growing throughout the war (North Carolina Shipbuilding Company, *Five Years of North Carolina Shipbuilding*, 8).

5. Accidents and injury rate from Scott, *Wilmington Shipyard*.

6. Interview of Robert S. Pollock by Wilbur D. Jones.

7. "Launching Culminates Years of Preparation."

8. Paid ad by Chamber of Commerce in special "Launching Edition" of Wilmington *Morning Star*, Dec. 6, 1941.

9. List of attendees at *Vance* launching from Crabtree, *Zebulon B. Vance*; details also reported in the Dec. 6, 1941, edition of the *Wilmington Star News*, "Launching Culminates Years of Preparation."

10. Twenty-one sunk by torpedoes, three lost to mines, three sunk by aerial bombardment. This does not count one lost to a mine after the war in 1947 or two that were used as breakwaters for the invasion of Normandy. From Scott, *The Wilmington Shipyard*, 75; Appendix I contains a list of all Wilmington Shipyard vessels and their dispositions.

11. Elverton Shands, interview by Jerry Parnell.

CHAPTER 2

1. Paul Brown, "The Story of Foggy Mountain Breakdown"; "Earl Scruggs

Biography: Chapter 1—The Early Years."

2. Barry R. Willis, "Earl Scruggs."

3. Kelley, *Thelonious Monk*, 23.

4. "Klook-Mop" Clarke from Kelley, *Thelonious Monk*, 60.

5. John S. Wilson, "Thelonious Monk Created Wry Jazz Melodies and New Harmonies."

6. Porter, *John Coltrane*, 37.

CHAPTER 3

1. "Fort Bragg History"; Joseph M. Herbert, interview by the author.

2. National Park Service, "Pope Air Force Base Historic District"; "Fort Bragg History."

3. Civilian Conservation Corps, *1936 Annual*.

4. "Fort Bragg History."

5. Thomas D. McCollum, interview by the author.

6. General William C. Lee Memorial Commission, *Commemorative Tribute*.

7. On display at the General William C. Lee Airborne Museum, Dunn, NC.

8. On display at 82nd Airborne Division Museum at Fort Bragg.

9. "Fort Bragg History."

10. All the preceding details about construction from Fort Bragg site visit to the old barracks and interview with Thomas D. McCollum.

11. *Paratroops* (film), 1943.

12. Thomas D. McCollum, interview and demonstration of jump protocol at the Fort Bragg training towers, Oct. 25, 2017.

13. "Fort Bragg History."

14. General William C. Lee Memorial Commission, *Commemorative Tribute*, and "History of the 101st Airborne Division (Air Assault)."

CHAPTER 4

1. From a now inactive NOAA web page and a now inactive NOAA Hurricane Research Division, Atlantic Oceanographic & Meteorological Laboratory web page (copies of original articles in author's possession).

2. Kenneth Reece, "75 Years Apart."

3. Sherrie Norris, "Granny Greene and the '40 Flood"; Ivery C. Greene, *A Disastrous Flood*, 53.

4. Greene, *A Disaastrous Flood*, 54, 2–3.

5. Anne C. Witt et al., "Life, Death and Landslides."

6. Norris, "Granny Greene and the '40 Flood"; and Greene, *A Disastrous Flood*.

7. Greene, *A Disastrous Flood*, 54 (I refer to her in the text as "Ivery" to differentiate her from all the other Greenes).

8. Greene, 67, 69, and 71.

9. Greene, 22.

10. Greene, 2–3 and 26.

11. Greene, 91.

12. Greene, 32–35.

13. Greene, 36–40.

14. Greene, 9–11.

15. "The Flood of Forty—Watauga's Worst Moment."

16. "Floods of 1916 and 1940."

17. Jesse Campbell. "A Look Back After 70 Years."

18. Sam Shumate, "Courting History."

19. "The Flood of Forty—Watauga's Worst Moment."

20. Greene, *A Disastrous Flood*, 5–6.

21. Dave Tabler, "North Carolina Ghost Town."

CHAPTER 5

1. Cherokee Preservation Foundation, "Who We Are."

2. Cherokee Nation Cultural Resource Center, "A Brief History of the Trail of Tears."

3. Leonard Carson Lambert, as told to Michael Lambert, *Up From These Hills*, xx–xxi.

4. Anne Mitchell Whisnant, "Parkway Development and the Eastern Band of Cherokees," Part 1.

5. John R. Finger, *Cherokee Americans*, 77; Whisnant, "Parkway Development and the Eastern Band of Cherokees," Part 1; Lambert, 35.

6. Mattea V. Sanders, " 'I got to do something to keep my family up' "; wage amount cited in Lambert, 42.

7. Clyde M. Blair to Commissioner of Indian Affairs D. E. Murphy, February 20, 1940, cited in Sanders, " 'I got to do something to keep my family up.' "

8. Finger, *Cherokee Americans*, 105; Lambert, *Up From These Hills*, 21.

9. Whisnant, "Parkway Development," Part 1.

10. Harold L. Ickes, "Message to the Cherokee Tribe," cited in Whisnant, Part 1, 1.

11. Whisnant, Part 2.

12. Finger, *Cherokee Americans*, 99–100 and 88–97.

13. Finger, 96.

14. Whisnant, Part 3.

15. Finger, *Cherokee Americans*, 108-9.

16. Finger, 111–12.

17. Lambert, *Up From These Hills*, 190–91.

18. Finger, *Cherokee Americans*, 115–17; also Cecelia Moore, "Outdoor Dramas."

CHAPTER 6

1. Gary R. Grant, interview by the author, June 13, 2017, and September 6, 2017.

2. "Florenza Moore Grant and Matthew Grant" (obituary).

3. Jess Gilbert and Spencer D. Wood, "Experiments in Land Reform and Racial Justice"; Donald Holley, "The Negro in the New Deal Resettlement Program."

4. Clarence A. Wiley, "Settlement and Unsettlement in the Resettlement Administration Program," 457–58.

5. Gilbert and Wood, "Experiments in Land Reform and Racial Justice"; Gilbert and Wood put the number of all-Black projects at nine, but other sources generally cite thirteen.

6. Gary R. Grant, interview by author.

7. Gilbert and Wood, "Experiments in Land Reform and Racial Justice," 9.

8. Interview with Gary R. Grant, no. U-0773, Southern Oral History Program Collection, 2.

9. Dustin Renwick, "Rosenwald Schools."

10. Gary R. Grant, interview by the author.

11. Interview with Gary R. Grant, no. U-0466, Southern Oral History Program Collection, 19.

12. Gary R. Grant, interview by the author.

13. Interview with Gary R. Grant, no. U-0466, Southern Oral History Program Collection, 3.

14. Gary R. Grant, interview by author.

CHAPTER 7

1. "June 1, 1944."

2. Sophie Ochmann and Max Roser, "Polio"; and World Health Organization, "Poliomyelitis."

3. "Doctors Directing Polio War Are Impressive Lot, From Far and Near,"

Greensboro Daily News, August 11, 1944 (as quoted in Sink, *The Grit Behind the Miracle*).

4. World Health Organization, "Poliomyelitis."

5. David M. Oshinsky, *Polio,* 25–27.

6. Sink, 71.

7. The account of the meeting between the three doctors and the subsequent construction of the facility is based largely on Sink, 24–33 and 44, with other details from Hickory Museum of Art, "The 'Miracle of Hickory.' "

8. "Dr. Hahn's Parked Automobile 'Miracle of Hickory' Symbol," *Hickory Daily Record,* Aug. 7, 1958 (cited in Sink, *The Grit Behind the Miracle,* 41).

9. Sink, 73–74.

10. Greensboro information and quotes from Jordan Green, "1948 Polio Epidemic."

11. Hickory Museum of Art, "The 'Miracle of Hickory.' "

12. Sink, *The Grit Behind the Miracle,* 15.

CHAPTER 8

1. The account of Juanita Shook's encounter with the TVA man based on interview with Juanita Shook Lester by the author.

2. David Monteith, "The Creation of the Great Smoky Mountain National Park."

3. Lance Holland, *Fontana,* 203-4.

4. Previous paragraphs based on interview with Earl Kirkland by the author.

5. Holland, *Fontana,* 155 and 204.

6. Holland, 155–61.

7. Interview with John Barton by the author.

8. Interview with Jeanne Huggins Reavis by the author.

9. Wanda Presswood's accounts from interview with Wanda Presswood Newman by the author.

10. Holland, *Fontana,* 179.

11. Interview with Paul Banks by the author.

12. Holland, *Fontana,* 162–65.

13. Tennessee Valley Authority, "Fontana Dam," précis of *The Fontana Project,* 1945, and *The Fontana Project* (film), 1942.

CHAPTER 9

1. H. C. Sumner, "The North Atlantic of September 8–16, 1944," 187.

2. *Rocky Mount Evening Telegram*, Sept. 12, 1944, 1.

3. Ken Adams, "The Great Atlantic Hurricane of September 1944."

4. "Morehead City and Beaufort Isolated by the Hurricane."

5. United Press International, Sept. 14, 1944.

6. John Hairr, *Great Hurricanes of North Carolina*, 118–19.

7. Hairr, 106, 107.

8. Bill Sharpe, quoted from *The State* in Hair, 120.

9. "Hurricane Does Heavy Damage in Eastern N.C."

10. Neel Keller, " 'Cape Hatteras Boy' looks back on the banks in the 1940s," and *Life* magazine, June 16, 1947.

11. "Coast Guard Cutter Speeds More Supplies for Villages along North Carolina Shore," Associated Press, filed from Burlington and carried by the *Burlington Daily Times-News*, Sept. 21, 1944, 2.

12. "Only Two Houses Left Standing in Rodanthe."

13. Hairr, 121.

14. "Hurricane Does Heavy Damage in Eastern N.C."

15. Accounts of the sinking of the *Bledsoe* and the *Jackson* from United States Coast Guard, press release, Sept. 18, 1944.

16. Hairr, 121, 122.

17. Associated Press, Elizabeth City, Sept. 16, 1944; "Coast Guard Cutter Speeds More Supplies."

18. "Coast Guard Cutter Speeds More Supplies."

19. Charles B. Carney and Albert V. Hardy, *North Carolina Hurricanes*, 27.-1.

20. Associated Press, Elizabeth City, Sept. 16, 1944.

21. Sumner, 188.

22. Adams, "The Great Atlantic Hurricane of September 1944."

CHAPTER 10

1. Wages per Nannie M. Tilley, *The R. J. Reynolds Tobacco Company*, 376–77; Getty Images, video, 1942.

2. Robert Rodgers Korstad, *Civil Rights Unionism*, 17. Also cited from interview with Theodosia Simpson Phelps by Robert Rodgers Korstad, no. E-0151, Southern Oral History Program Collection, 4.

3. Akosua Barthwell. "Trade Unionism in North Carolina."

4. Korstad, 17–18.

5. Tilley, 378; interview with Theodosia Simpson Phelps by Robert Rodgers Korstad, no. E-0151, Southern Oral History Program Collection.

6. Tilley, 396 (number of gates).

7. Account of the events of June 17, 1943, per Korstad, 14, and Tilley, 378–79; the interviews with Simpson and McClendon from Korstad, 17–23.

8. Korstad, 196.

9. Details on Black per Korstad, 90.

10. Hugh Talmadge Lefler and Albert Ray Newsome, *North Carolina*, 643.

11. Korstad, *Civil Rights Unionism*, 30–31.

12. Tilley, *The R. J. Reynolds Tobacco Company*, 383–85 and 410.

13. Tilley, 395.

14. H.B. 229, Chapter 328, session laws and resolutions passed by the General Assembly (1947), 381, https://digital.ncdcr.gov/digital/collection/p249901coll22/id/251322.

CHAPTER 11

1. Martin Duberman, *Black Mountain*, 19–20; Mary Emma Harris, *The Arts at Black Mountain College*, 2, 30–31.

2. The discussion of art, based on text and illustrations, per Vincent Katz (ed.), *Black Mountain College*, 15, 20–21, 39–44, 53–54, 133–45, and 146–52.

3. Duberman, *Black Mountain*, 34, 49.

4. National Park Service, "Black Mountain College Historic District."

5. Black Mountain College Project, "Alfred Lawrence Kocher" and "The Decision to Move to Lake Eden."

6. Mervin Lane (ed.), *Black Mountain College*, 80–81.

7. Duberman, *Black Mountain*, 155, 162.

8. Radin career information per David H. Price, *Threatening Anthropology*, 200–202.

9. Duberman, *Black Mountain*, 211–12, 165

10. Lane, *Black Mountain College*, 83 and 89.

11. Duberman, *Black Mountain*, 223.

12. Wiley J. Williams and Robert Blair Vocci, "Black Mountain College", 1.

CHAPTER 12

1. Details of the aerial survey from United States Marine Corps, Cultural Resources Management, "History of Camp Lejeune."

2. Tomas J. Farnham, "Camp Lejeune"; Ronald A. Culp, *The First Black United States Marines*, 31.

3. Culp, 25.

4. Colonel Mary V. Stremlow, USMCR (Ret), "Training" and "Overseas."

5. John S. Duvall, "North Carolina's Wartime Miracle."

6. National Security Act of 1957, cited in Ian Padden, *U.S. Marines*, 10–11.

7. Culp, *The First Black United States Marines*, 16–17.

8. *Southern Pines Pilot*, Sept. 1, 1950.

9. Culp, *The First Black United States Marines*, 20, 21, 24–25, 29.

10. Melton Alonza McLaurin, *The Marines of Montford Point*, 49, 50.

11. McLaurin, 129, 140, 151, and 152–53

CHAPTER 13

1. David Leroy Corbitt (ed.), *Public Addresses, Letters, and Papers of Joseph Melville Broughton*, vii, ix.

2. "Broughton to Become Governor with Few Definite Commitments."

3. Quotes and details from the text of Broughton's inaugural are from Corbitt, *Public Addresses*, 7–8.

4. Quote and crowd estimate from "New Governor Inaugurated at Raleigh Jan. 9."

5. Details of groups he addressed from a variety of newspapers; dynamite demonstration from "Highway Commission Opens Lime Mine in Yadkin County."

6. "North Carolina's 'First Lady' Speaks Out for Cotton."

7. William T. Moye, "Broughton, Joseph."

8. William Tuck, "Governor Urges Graduates," 1.

9. J. Melville Broughton, "Report to the People," Dec. 30, 1944, in Corbitt, 390.

10. John Robert Moore, "Bailey, Josiah William."

11. "Rites Are Set for Broughton in Afternoon."

12. Ruth Lenkoski, "Views Differ on Graham's New Position."

13. "Scott Believes Newest Solon Is 'Best Man.' "

SELECTED SOURCES

ARCHIVAL PAPERS (UNPUBLISHED)

Edwards, Jennifer. "A Color Line in the Sand: African American Seaside Leisure in New Hanover County, North Carolina." Master's thesis, University of North Carolina Wilmington, 2003.

Gilbert, Jess, and Spencer D. Wood. "Experiments in Land Reform and Justice: The New Deal State and Local African-Americans Remake Civil Society in the Rural South, 1935–2004." ResearchGate. https://www .researchgate.net/publication/242776852. Originally presented at the Rural Sociological Society Annual Meeting, August 2004, Sacramento, CA, and at the Association of Public Policy and management Annual Meeting, November 2003, Washington, DC; revised by the author December 8, 2014.

Monteith, David. "The Creation of the Great Smoky Mountain National Park from Historical Trauma to Hope and Healing." Undated. Swain County Heritage Museum, Bryson City, NC. Mr. Monteith was a Swain County Commissioner.

Radin, Paul. "Paul Radin Papers: Provenance, Biographical Note, Scope and Content." Marquette University Archives. http://www.marquette.edu/ library/archives/Mss/PR/PR-sc.php.

Roosevelt, Franklin D. Executive Order 7027, Establishing the Resettlement Administration, May 1, 1935. *The American Presidency Project*. https://www.presidency.ucsb.edu/documents/executive-order-7027-establishing-the-resettlement-administration.

Windle, Charles D., Joseph S. Ward, Kimball Nedved, and Jerome Nathan. "The Effect of Mock Tower Height in Airborne Training." Human Research Unit Nr 3, CONARC, Fort Benning, GA, under the technical supervision of the George Washington University Human Resources Research Office, operating under contract with the Department of the Army, 1956.

ARCHIVES & ORGANIZATIONS

82d Airborne Division War Memorial Museum, Fort Bragg, N.C.
Airborne & Special Operations Museum, Fayetteville, N.C.
Earl Scruggs Center, Shelby, N.C.
Federal Point History Center, Carolina Beach, N.C.
Fontana Dam & Visitors Center, Fontana, N.C.

Fontana Village Resort, Fontana, N.C.

Fort Bragg Public Affairs Office, Fort Bragg, N.C.

General William C. Lee Airborne Museum, Dunn, N.C.

The History House, Concerned Citizens of Tillery, Tillery, N.C.

Museum of the Cherokee Indian, Cherokee, N.C.

Swain County Visitors Center and Heritage Museum, Bryson City, N.C.

University of North Carolina at Chapel Hill, Louis Round Wilson Library Special Collections, including *Documenting the American South*

University of North Carolina Wilmington, Archives and Special Collections, William Madison Randall Library

Wilson Creek Visitor Center (Caldwell County), Collettsville, N.C.

ARTICLES

82d Airborne Division War Memorial Museum. "The 82d Airborne Division: History." http://www.82ndairbornedivisionmuseum.com/general-information/.

Adams, Ken. "The Great Atlantic Hurricane of September 1944: My Remembrances." *Destroyer Escort Sailors Association*, May 2008.

Ahearn, Lorraine. "Strike: When Workers Broke Camel City." *Greensboro News & Record*, Feb. 28, 2009. http://www.greensboro.com/news/columnists/strike-when-workers-broke-camel-city/article_4438e49b-569d-53d7-8ac2-9602936514b6.html.

Associated Press, from *Burlington Daily Times-News*. "Coast Guard Cutter Speeds More Supplies for Villages Along North Carolina Shore." Sept. 21, 1944, p. 2.

Bartenstein, Fred. "Earl Scruggs Biography." Bluegrass Music Hall of Fame. https://www.bluegrasshall.org/inductees/earl-scruggs/#biography.

Barthwell, Akosua. "Trade Unionism in North Carolina: The Strike Against Reynolds Tobacco, 1947." Rutgers University, Occasional Paper No. 21 (1977). https://archive.org/stream/TradeUnionismNorthCarolina/TradeUnionismNorthCarolina_djvu.txt.

"Billy Conn to Fight in Winston-Salem." *Wilkesboro Journal-Patriot*, Sept. 4, 1941. http://newspapers.digitalnc.org/lccn/sn85042127/1941-09-04/ed-1/seq-6/#index=19&rows=20&proxtext=J.+Melville+Broughton&searchType=basic&sequence=0&words=Broughton+J+Melville&page=12.

Black Mountain College Project. "Alfred Lawrence Kocher." http://www.blackmountaincollegeproject.org/Biographies/KOCHER%20LAWRENCE/KOCHER%20LAWRENCE%20BIO.htm.

Black Mountain College Project. "The Decision to Move to Lake Eden." http://www .blackmountaincollegeproject.org/ARCHITECTURE/ CAMPUSES/LAKE%20EDEN/NEW%20BUILDINGS/24%20A%20 STUDIES%20BUILDING%20TEXT.htm.

Black Mountain Museum and Arts Center. "FBI Investigations at BMC." http://www.blackmountaincollege.org/fbi-investigations-bmc/.

"Broughton to Become Governor with Few Definite Commitments." *Waynesville Mountaineer*, June 27, 1940, p. 9. https://newspapers.digitalnc .org/lccn/sn92074106/1940-06-27/ed-1/seq-9/.

Brown, Paul. "The Story of 'Foggy Mountain Breakdown' " (broadcast with transcript). *Weekend Edition*, National Public Radio, April 1, 2000. http://www.npr.org/2000/04/01/1072355/npr-100-earl-scruggs.

Cabarrus College of Health Sciences. "History." https://www.carolinas healthcare.org/education/cabarrus-college-of-health-sciences/about-us/ History.

Campbell, Jesse. "A Look Back After 70 Years: The Disastrous Flood of 1940." *Ashe Mountain Times*, Aug. 27, 2010. http://ashemountaintimes .com/community/a-look-back-after-years-the-disastrous-flood-of/article_ 001ad5fb-d754-5be8-b7ab-0242ef821807.html.

Carolina Music Ways Music Heritage Resource Group. "The Rise of Radio Stations in the North Carolina Piedmont," 2003 (from a now inactive web page; original article in author's possession).

Cherokee Nation Cultural Resource Center. "A Brief History of the Trail of Tears." https://www.pcs.org/features/a-brief-history-of-the-trail-of-tears

Cherokee Preservation Foundation. "Who We Are." http://cherokee preservation.org/who-we-are/about-the-ebci/.

Duvall, John S. "North Carolina's Wartime Miracle: Defending the Nation." NCpedia, reprinted from *Tar Heel Junior Historian*, 47, no. 2 (Spring 2008). https://www.ncpedia.org/anchor/north-carolinas-wartime.

"Earl Scruggs Biography: Chapter 1—The Early Years." https://earlscruggs .com/biography.html.

Elliott, Marvin L. "The 'Miracle' of Hickory: Mass Media and the 'Miracle.' " https://www.ndsu.edu/pubweb/~rcollins/elliott.htm.

Elliston, John. "FBI Investigation of Black Mountain College Revealed in Newly Released File." *Carolina Public Press*, Aug. 5, 2015.

Erickson, Mark St. John. "Shipbuilding Boss Homer L. Ferguson Shaped Yard and Region." *The Daily Press*, July 18, 2015. https://www.dailypress. com/history/dp-nws-ferguson-20150718-story.html.

Eyewitness to History. "The Bonus Army." http ://www.eyewitness tohistory.com/snprelief4.htm.

"Famous Baptist Church of Durham Holds Celebration." *The Carolina Times*, Oct. 4, 1941. https://newspapers.digitalnc.org/lccn/sn83045120/1941-10-04/ed-1/seq-1/#words=Baptist+Church+Famous.

Farnham, Tomas J. "Camp Lejeune." *The Encyclopedia of North Carolina*, edited by William S. Powell. Chapel Hill: University of North Carolina Press, 2006.

"The Flood of Forty—Watauga's Worst Moment." Carolina Corner. http://www.carolinacorner.com/attractions/flood-forty-wataugas-worst-moment.htm (now inactive; copy of original article in author's possession).

"Floods of 1916 and 1940." DigitalHeritage.org, Western Carolina University. https://digitalheritage.org/2010/08/floods-of-1916-and-1940/.

"Florenza Moore Grant and Matthew Grant" (obituary). *The Daily Herald*, Jan. 18, 2002.

"Fort Bragg History." https://home.army.mil/bragg/index.php/about/fort-bragg-history.

Gilbert, Jess, and Spencer D. Wood. "Experiments in Land Reform and Racial Justice: The New Deal State and Local African-Americans Remake Civil Society in the Rural South, 1935–2004." https://www.researchgate.net/publication/242776852. Originally presented at the Rural Sociological Society Annual Meeting, August 2004, Sacramento, CA, and at the Association of Public Policy and Management Annual Meeting, November 2003, Washington, DC; revised by the author Dec. 8, 2014.

Goldsmith, Thomas. " 'Foggy Mountain Breakdown'—Lester Flatt and Earl Scruggs (1949)." Library of Congress. https://www.loc.gov/programs/static/national-recording-preservation-board/documents/FoggyMtBreakdown.pdf.

Gould, Tony. *A Summer Plague: Polio and Its Survivors*. New Haven, CT: Yale University Press, 1995.

Green, Jordan. "1948 Polio Epidemic." *Yes! Weekly*, April 1, 2008.

Gussow, Mel. "Julius Monk, Cabaret Impresario, Dies at 82. *New York Times* (obituary), Aug. 22, 1995.

Harris, Craig. "Charlie Monroe Artist Biography." *AllMusic*. https://www.allmusic.com/artist/charlie-monroe-mn0000807457/biography.

Hickory Museum of Art. "The 'Miracle of Hickory': The 1944 Polio Hospital." April 7, 2015. https://www.hickoryart.org/blog/2015/04/08/2015-4-7-the-miracle-of-hickory-the-1944-polio-hospital.

"Highway Commission Opens Lime Mine in Yadkin County." *Wilksboro Journal Patriot*, Jan. 25, 1943, p. 1. https://newspapers.digitalnc.org/lccn/sn85042127/1943-01-25/ed-1/seq-1/.

"History of the 101st Airborne Division (Air Assault)." 101st Airborne Division Association. https://screamingeagle.org/division-history/.

Holley, Donald. "The Negro in the New Deal Resettlement Program." *Agricultural History*, Agricultural History Society, vol. 45, no. 3 (July 1971), 179–93. https://www.jstor.org/stable/pdf/3741977.pdf?refreqid=excelsior%3Aab29aef9e3f4946c88107fa3a968fedf.

Holt, John B. "An Analysis of Methods and Criteria Used in Selecting Families for Colonization Projects." Social Research Report No. 1. Washington, DC: United States Department of Agriculture, 1937.

"House Leader May Lash Out at Isolation." *The Daily Tar Heel*, May 24, 1941, p. 1. https://newspapers.digitalnc.org/lccn/sn92073228/1941-05-24/ed-1/seq-1/#words=House+Lash+Leader+May+Out.

Hurd, Charles. "Reuben James Hit." *New York Times*, Nov. 1, 1941, p. 1.

"Hurricane Does Heavy Damage in Eastern N.C." *Statesville Record and Landmark*, Sept. 16, 1944, p. 1.

Jack, Emily. "WVT Charlotte in the Golden Age of Radio." NCPedia. https://www.ncpedia.org/anchor/wbt-charlotte-golden-age.

"June 1, 1944: First Case of Polio Diagnosed in Catawba County." WFMY News 2, June 1, 2016. https://www.wfmynews2.com/article/features/june-1-1944-first-case-of-polio-diagnosed-in-catawba-county/83-226370126.

Klara, Robert. "FDR: The Long Goodbye" (excerpt from *FDR's Funeral Train: A Betrayed Widow, a Soviet Spy, and a Presidency in the Balance*). *Atlanta*, Aug. 2, 2010. http://www.atlantamagazine.com/history/fdr-the-long-goodbye1/.

Klara, Robert. "FDR's Funeral Train." *The History Reader*, June 23, 2011. (excerpt from *FDR's Funeral Train: A Betrayed Widow, a Soviet Spy, and a Presidency in the Balance*). https://www.thehistoryreader.com/us-history/fdrs-funeral-train/.

Keller, Neel. " 'Cape Hatteras Boy' Looks Back on the Banks in the 1940s." *Outer Banks Sentinal*, Dec. 14, 2011.

Larsen, Eric. "Shore Battered by Hurricane of 1944: Towns in Ruin This Week 73 Years Ago." *Cherry Hill (NJ) Courier Post*, Sept. 11, 2017, p. A5.

"Launching Culminates Years of Preparation." *Wilmington Morning Star*, Dec. 6, 1941.

Lenkoski, Ruth. "Views Differ on Graham's New Position." *The Salemite*,

April 1, 1949. http://newspapers.digitalnc.org/lccn/2015236777/1949-04-01/ ed-1/seq-1/#index=16&rows=20&words=Broughton+J+Melville&searchType =basic&sequence=0&proxtext=J.+Melville+Broughton&page=11.

"*Life* Visits Cape Hatteras." *Life*, June 16, 1947, pp. 133–37.

Martin, Stephen. "Striking Out Against Big Tobacco." *Duke Magazine*, March 31, 2004. https://alumni.duke.edu/magazine/articles/striking-out-against-big-tobacco.

McFee, Philip, and Wiley J. Williams. "Radio Enters Its 'Golden Age' in North Carolina." *Encyclopedia of North Carolina*, edited by William S. Powell. Chapel Hill: University of North Carolina Press, 2006. https://www .ncpedia.org/part-2-radio-enters-its-golden-age-.

Moore, Cecelia (with additional research by Ronnie W. Faulkner, Ron Holland, and Richard L. Zuber). "Outdoor Dramas." NCPedia, 2006. https:// www.ncpedia.org/outdoor-dramas.

Moore, John Robert. "Bailey, Josiah William." *Dictionary of North Carolina Biography*, Vol. 1. Edited by William S. Powell. Chapel Hill: University of North Carolina Press, 1979. https://www.ncpedia.org/ biography/bailey-josiah-william.

"Morehead City and Beaufort Isolated by the Hurricane." *Statesville Record and Landmark*, Sept. 14, 1944.

Moye, William T. "Broughton, Joseph." NCPedia. https://www.ncpedia .org/biography/broughton-joseph-melville.

National Park Service. "Black Mountain College Historic District." National Register of Historic Places Travel Itinerary. https://www.nps.gov/ nr/travel/asheville/bla.htm.

National Park Service. "Pope Air Force Base Historic District." https:// www.nps.gov/articles/pope-air-force-base-historic-district.htm.

NCDNR. "Polio Outbreak and the 'Miracle of Hickory.' " https ://www .ncdcr.gov/blog/2016/06/01/polio-outbreak-and-the-miracle-of-hickory.

NCPedia. "The GI Bill." https://www.ncpedia.org/anchor/gi-bill.

"New Governor Inaugurated at Raleigh Jan. 9." *Wilkesboro Journal-Patriot*, Jan. 13, 1941, p. 7. https://newspapers.digitalnc.org/lccn/sn85042127 /1941-01-13/ed-1/seq-7/.

Nipp, Robert E. "The Negro in the New Deal Resettlement Program: A Comment." *Agricultural History* 45, no. 3 (July 1971): 195–200. http://www .jstor.org/stable/3741979.

Norris, Sherrie. "Granny Greene and the '40 Flood." *Watauga Democrat*, Nov. 15, 2015. http://www.wataugademocrat.com/community/granny-

greene-and-the-flood/article_61a84eac-2203-5c33-91f3-eb5c96d2a30b.
html.

"North Carolina's 'First Lady' Speaks Out for Cotton; Portrait Appears in
National Series." *Raeford News Journal*, Oct. 21, 1943. http://newspapers
.digitalnc.org/lccn/sn93064776/1943-10-21/ed-1/seq-4/#index=5&rows=20
&words=Broughton+J+Melville&searchType=basic&sequence=0&proxtext=J
.+Melville+Broughton&page=5.

Novak, Matt. "We Got Buckminster Fuller's FBA File." *Gizmodo*, May
20, 2015. https://paleofuture.gizmodo.com/we-got-buckminster-fullers-fbi-
file-1704777475.

Ochmann, Sophie, and Max Roser. "Polio." *Our World in Data*, Nov. 9,
2017. https://ourworldindata.org/polio.

"Only Two Houses Left Standing in Rodanthe; All But 12 Houses
Destroyed Within Avon." *Rocky Mount Evening Telegram*, Sept. 18, 1944, p. 1.

Osment, Timothy N. "Floods of 1916 and 1940." https://digitalheritage
.org/2010/08/floods-of-1916-and-1940/.

Reece, Kenneth. "75 Years Apart—1940s Flood Anniversary Noted,
Downtown Boone Aug. 1940/Downtown Boone Aug. 2015." Watauga Online.
http://wataugaonline.com/75-years-apart-1940s-flood-anniversary-noted-
downtown-boone-aug-1940-downtown-boone-aug-2015/.

Renwick, Dustin. "Rosenwald Schools: Rediscovered Education."
The Daily Herald, July 22, 2012. https://www.rrdailyherald.com/news/
rosenwald-schools-rediscovered-education/article_7697039e-189d-53d6-
9c33-d2157e043b37.html.

"Rites Are Set for Broughton in Afternoon." *The Daily Tarheel*, March 8,
1949, p. 1. https://newspapers.digitalnc.org/lccn/sn92073228/1949-03-08/
ed-1/seq-1/#words=Broughton+BROUGHTON+Rites+Set.

Sanders, Mattea V. " 'I got to do something to keep my family up': The
CCC-Indian Division Offers a New Deal for the Eastern Band of Cherokees."
https://www.archives.gov/files/publications/prologue/2014/winter/ccc-
cherokee.pdf.

"Scott Believes Newest Solon Is 'Best Man.' "*Daily Tar Heel*, March 25,
1949, p. 1. https://newspapers.digitalnc.org/lccn/sn92073228/1949-03-25/
ed-1/seq-1/.

Sears, David. "Going Long: The 2nd Maine Raiders' Legendary March
Across Guadalanal." *World War II Magazine*, Aug. 14, 2016.

"Ship Ahoy! Wilmington Goes Ahead." *Wilmington Morning Star*, Nov.
9, 1941.

Shumate, Sam. "Courting History: Remembering the 1940 Flood." *Jefferson Post*, Aug. 11, 2016.

Silverstein, Judy. "Adrift: Coast Guard Cutter Jackson." United States Coast Guard: 2006. http://www.navyandmarine.org/ondeck/USRCS_Adrift.htm.

Stremlow, Colonel Mary V., USMCR (Ret). "Training: Camp Lejeune" and "Overseas." *FREE A MARINE TO FIGHT: Women Marines in World War II*. National Park Service: Marines in World War II Commemorative Series. https://www.nps.gov/parkhistory/online_books/npswapa/extContent/usmc/pcn-190-003129-00/sec5.htm.

Sumner, H. C. "The North Atlantic of September 8–16, 1944." *Monthly Weather Review*, National Weather Bureau, Dec. 5, 1944.

Tabler, Dave. "North Carolina Ghost Town." http://www.appalachian history.net/2015/05/north-carolina-ghost-town.html.

Tuck, William. "Governor Urges Graduates at N.C. College for Negroes to Avoid Dangers of Atrophy." *Carolina Times*, June 7, 1941. https://newspapers.digitalnc.org/lccn/sn83045120/1941-06-07/ed-1/seq-1/.

United States Marine Corps, Cultural Resources Management. "History of Camp Lejeune." https://www.lejeune.marines.mil/Offices-Staff/Environmental-Mgmt/Cultural-Resources/History-Live/History-of-Camp-Lejeune/.

Vannoy, Allyn. "Expanding the Size of the U.S. Military in World War II." *Warfare History*, June 26, 2017.

Whisnant, Anne Mitchell. "Parkway Development and the Eastern Band of Cherokees" (3 parts). *DocSouth* https://docsouth.unc.edu/blueridge parkway/overlooks/cherokee-1/.

Wiley, Clarence A. "Settlement and Unsettlement in the Resettlement Administration Program." *Law and Contemporary Problems* 4 (1937): 456–72. https://scholarship.law.duke.edu/lcp/vol4/iss4/4.

Williams, Wiley J., and Robert Blair Vocci. "Black Mountain College." In *Encyclopedia of North Carolina*, edited by William S. Powell. Chapel Hill: University of North Carolina Press, 2006.

Willis, Barry R. "Earl Scruggs." https://flatt-and-scruggs.com/earlbio.html.

Wilmington Morning Star. Paid ad by Chamber of Commerce in special "Launching Edition." Dec. 6, 1941.

Wilson, John S. "Thelonious Monk Created Wry Jazz Melodies and New Harmonies." *New York Times* (obituary), Feb. 18, 1982.

Winekam, Mark. "Yesterday: A Flower Wreath for FDR's Train." *Salisbury Post*, Feb. 19, 2018. http://m.salisburypost.com/2018/02/19/yesterday-a-flower-wreath-for-fdrs-train/.

Witt, Anne. C., et al. "Life, Death and Landslides: The August 13–14, 1940, Storm Event in Watauga County, North Carolina." *Geological Society of America Abstracts with Programs* 39, no. 2 (2007): 76 (presented at Southeastern Section Annual Meeting in Savannah, GA, March 29–30, 2007).

World Health Organization. "Poliomyelitis: Fact Sheet." April 2017. http://www.who.int/mediacentre/factsheets/fs114/en/.

BOOKS

Ambrose, Stephen. *Band of Brothers: E Company, 506th Regiment, 101st Airborne from Normandy to Hitler's Eagle's Nest*. New York: Touchstone/ Simon & Schuster, 1992.

Badger, Anthony J. *North Carolina and the New Deal*. Raleigh: North Carolina Division of Archives and History, 1981.

———. *Prosperity Road: The New Deal, Tobacco, and North Carolina*. Chapel Hill: University of North Carolina Press, 1980.

Best, Mary (ed.). *North Carolina's Shining Hour: Images and Voices from World War II*. Greensboro: Our State North Carolina Books, 2005.

Cheatham, James T. *The Atlantic Turkey Shoot: U-Boats Off the Outer Banks in World War II*. Greenville, NC: Williams and Simpson, 1990.

Civilian Conservation Corps. *1936 Annual, Civilian Conservation Corps Camps in District Two, Third Corps Area*. http://www.justinmuseum.com/ jkjustin2/d23c4.html.

Conley, Robert J. *A Cherokee Encyclopedia*. Albuquerque: University of New Mexico Press, 2007.

Corbitt, David Leroy (ed.). *Public Addresses, Letters, and Papers of Joseph Melville Broughton, Governor of North Carolina, 1941–1945*. Raleigh: North Carolina State Division of Archives and History, 1950.

Crews, J. Marshall. *From These Beginnings: Wilmington College, 1946–1969*, edited by Mary Duex Dodson. The Publishing Laboratory of the Department of Creative Writing, University of North Carolina Wilmington, 1984 and 2001.

Culp, Ronald A. *The First Black United States Marines: The Men of Montford Point, 1942–1946*. Jefferson, NC: MacFarland, 2007.

Dew, Stephen Herman. *The Queen City at War: Charlotte, North Carolina, During World War II, 1939–1945*. New York: University Press of America, 2001.

Duberman, Martin. *Black Mountain: An Exploration in Community*. New York: E. P. Dutton, 1972.

Finger, John R. *Cherokee Americans: The Eastern Band of the Cherokees in the Twentieth Century.* Lincoln: University of Nebraska Press, 1991.

General William C. Lee Memorial Commission. *Commemorative Tribute: Excerpts of the Life and History of General William C. Lee, the American Airborne, and Glider Planes.* Dunn, NC: General William C. Lee Airborne Museum, 2003.

Gilbert, Edward. *US Marine Corps Raider 1942–43.* New York: Osprey Publishing, 2006.

Gould, Tony. *A Summer Plague: Polio and Its Survivors.* New Haven, CT: Yale University Press, 1995.

Greene, Ivery C. *A Disastrous Flood: A True and Fascinating Story.* Richmond, VA: William Byrd Press, 1941.

Hairr, John. *The Great Hurricanes of North Carolina.* Charleston, SC: The History Press, 2008.

Harris, Mary Emma. *The Arts at Black Mountain College.* Cambridge, MA: MIT Press, n.d.

———. *Remembering Black Mountain College.* Black Mountain Museum and Arts Center, 1996.

Holland, Lance. *Fontana: A Pocket History of Appalachia.* Robbinsville, NC: Appalachian History Series, 2001.

Huber, Patrick. *The Linthead Stomp: The Creation of Country Music in the Piedmont South.* Chapel Hill: University of North Carolina Press, 2008.

Jeffries, John W. *Wartime America: The World War II Home Front.* Chicago: Ivan R. Dee, 1996.

Jones, Wilbur D., Jr. *A Sentimental Journey: Memoirs of a Wartime Boomtown.* Shippensburg, PA, White Mane Books, 2002.

Katz, Vincent (ed.). *Black Mountain College: Experiment in Art.* Cambridge, MA: MIT Press, 2013.

Kelley, Robin D. G. *Thelonious Monk: The Life and Times of an American Original.* New York: Free Press, 2009.

Korstad, Robert Rodgers. *Civil Rights Unionism: Tobacco Workers and the Struggle for Democracy in the Mid-Twentieth-Century South.* Chapel Hill: University of North Carolina Press, 2003.

Lambert, Leonard Carson, as told to Michael Lambert. *Up From These Hills: Memories of a Cherokee Boyhood.* Lincoln: University of Nebraska Press, 2011.

Lane, Frederic C. *Ships for Victory: A History of Shipbuilding under the United States Maritime Commission in World War II.* Baltimore, MD: Johns

Hopkins University Press, 1951.

Lane, Mervin (ed.). *Black Mountain College: Sprouted Seeds—An Anthology of Personal Accounts*. Knoxville: University of Tennessee Press, 1990.

Lefler, Hugh Talmadge, and Albert Ray Newsome. *North Carolina: The History of a Southern State* (3rd edition). Chapel Hill: University of North Carolina Press, 1973.

Lemmon, Sarah McCulloh. *North Carolina's Role in World War II*. Raleigh, NC: North Carolina Division of Archives and History, 1964.

McLaurin, Melton Alonza. *The Marines of Montford Point: America's First Black Marines*. Chapel Hill: University of North Carolina Press, 2007.

Mooney, James. *Historical Sketch of the Cherokee*. Washington, DC: Smithsonian Institution Press, 1975.

Oshinsky, David M. *Polio: An American Story*. New York: Oxford University Press, 2005.

Padden, Ian. *U.S. Marines: From Boot Camp to the Battle Zones*. New York: Bantam, 1985.

Porter, Lewis. *John Coltrane: His Life and Music*. Ann Arbor: University of Michigan Press, 1998.

Powell, William S. (ed.). *The Encyclopedia of North Carolina*. Chapel Hill: University of North Carolina Press, 2006.

Price, David. H. *Threatening Anthropology: McCarthyism and the FBI's Surveillance of Activist Anthropologists*. Durham, NC: Duke University Press, 2004.

Robert, Joseph C. *The Story of Tobacco in America*. New York: Alfred A. Knopf, 1949.

Savitt, Todd L. *Medicine and Slavery: The Diseases and Health Care of Blacks in Antebellum Virginia*. Champaign: University of Illinois Press, 1981.

Scott, Ralph. *The Wilmington Shipyard: Welding a Fleet for Victory in World War II*. Charleston, SC: The History Press, 2007.

Shell, Marc. *Polio and Its Aftermath*. Cambridge, MA: Harvard University Press, 2005.

Sink, Alice E. *The Grit Behind the Miracle*. New York: University Press of America, 1998.

Tilley, Nannie M. *The R. J. Reynolds Tobacco Company*. Chapel Hill: University of North Carolina Press, 1985.

Watson, Alan D. *Wilmington: Port of North Carolina*. Columbia: University of South Carolina Press, 1992.

Willis, Barry R. *America's Music: Bluegrass—A History of Bluegrass in the Words of Its Pioneers*. Franktown, CO: Pine Valley Music, 1992.

Wilson-Giarratano, Gail. *Carolina Bluegrass: A High Lonesome History*. Charleston, SC: The History Press, 2015.

FILMS

The Fontana Project. Tennessee Valley Authority, 1942.

Getty Images. Video, 1942: Durham, North Carolina: Ligget-Meyers Tobacco Company. "CU Stemmery machine grabbing tobacco leaves by stems, MS Tobacco leaves into machine, stems conveyor out of machine roller. MS Inspector checking leaf 'strip' w/ hands."

Parachutes: Construction and Types. U.S. Army Training Film I-536, 1942.

Paratroops. U.S. Office of War Information, 1943.

INTERVIEWS

Paul Banks of the "Fontana Dam Kids," by the author at Fontana, NC, October 19, 2017.

John Barton of the "Fontana Dam Kids," by the author at Fontana, NC, October 19, 2017.

Phillip Dresser, shipbuilder, "North Carolina's WWII Experience," PBS North Carolina, https://video.pbsnc.org/video/unc-tv-presents-north-carolinas-wwii-experience/.

Gary R. Grant, Executive Director, Concerned Citizens of Tillery, by the author, June 13, 2017, and September 6, 2017. Mr. Grant has collected oral histories and documents relating to Tillery for decades. He also curates History House at Tillery. Details of his family life and that of the Tillery community not attributed to other sources come from him.

Gary R. Grant, no. U-0466, Southern Oral History Program Collection (#4007), Southern Historical Collection, Louis Round Wilson Special Collection Library, University of North Carolina at Chapel Hill, August 6, 2003, http://dc.lib.unc.edu/cgi-bin/showfile.exe?CISOROOT=/sohp&CISOPTR=6196&filename=6241.pdf.

Gary R. Grant, no. U-0773, Southern Oral History Program Collection (#4007), Southern Historical Collection, Louis Round Wilson Special Collection Library, University of North Carolina at Chapel Hill, August 17, 2011, http://dc.lib.unc.edu/cdm/compoundobject/collection/sohp/id/18029/rec/1.

Joseph M. Herbert, Colorado State University Center for the Environmental Management of Military Lands Research Archaeologist, interview by the author at Fort Bragg, October 25, 2017.

Earl Kirkland, by the author at Bryson City, NC, October 18, 2017.

Juanita Shook Lester, by the author at Bryson City, NC, October 18, 2017.

Thomas D. McCollum, Fort Bragg Garrison Public Affairs Officer and 24-year veteran of the 82d Airborne, interview by the author at Fort Bragg, October 25, 2017.

Dwight Morrow of the "Fontana Dam Kids," by the author at Fontana, NC, October 19, 2017.

Theodosia Simpson Phelps, no. E-0151, Southern Oral History Program Collection (#4007), Southern Historical Collection, Louis Round Wilson Special Collection Library, University of North Carolina at Chapel Hill, April 19, 1979, https://dc.lib.unc.edu/cdm/compoundobject/collection/sohp/id/4308/rec/60.

Wanda Presswood Newman of the "Fontana Dam Kids," by the author at Fontana, NC, October 19, 2017.

Robert S. Pollock, by Wilbur D. Jones, Wilbur D. Jones papers, Oral History Project, Archives and Special Collections, William Madison Randall Library, University of North Carolina Wilmington.

Jeannie Huggins Revis of the "Fontana Dam Kids," by the author at Fontana, NC, October 19, 2017.

Elverton Shands, by Jerry Parnell, Archives and Special Collections, University of North Carolina Wilmington, February 12, 2010.

MANUAL

Static Line Parachuting Techniques and Training. Headquarters, Department of the Army, 2013.

PAMPHLETS

Crabtree, Beth G. *The Zebulon B. Vance: A United States Liberty Ship.* Raleigh: North Carolina State Department of Archives and History, 1956.

North Carolina Shipbuilding Company. *Five Years of North Carolina Shipbuilding.* Wilmington: North Carolina Shipbuilding Company, 1946.

REPORTS

Brown, Marvin A. "Research Report: Tools for Assessing the Significance and Integrity of North Carolina's Rosenwald Schools and Comprehensive Investigation of Rosenwald Schools in Edgecombe, Halifax, Johnston, Nash, Wayne, and Wilson Counties." Office of Human Environment, Project Development and Environmental Analysis Branch, North Carolina Department of Transportation and Federal Highway Administration,

December 2007.

Carney, Charles B., and Albert V. Hardy *North Carolina Hurricanes: A Listing and Description of Tropical Cyclones Which Have Affected the State.* U.S. Department of Commerce, Environmental Science Services Division, Weather Bureau; revised Aug. 1967.

Fuller, R. Buckminster. FBI File. https://www.scribd.com/document /265921728/Buckminster-Fuller-s-FBI-File-Part-1.

Tennessee Valley Authority. *The Fontana Project: A Comprehensive Report on the Planning, Design, Construction, and Initial Operations of the Fontana Project, Technical Report No. 12.* Issued by the Tennessee Valley Authority (TVA) in 1950, prepared, coauthored, and illustrated by 140 men and women.

United States Coast Guard. Press release. Norfolk, VA, Sept. 18, 1944. Reprinted at https://www.ibiblio.org/hyperwar/USN/ships/tande/WSC/ wsc142-pr.html.

Veterans Affairs. "GI Bill History." https://veteranseducationsuccess.org/ gi-bill-history.

WEBSITES

Carolina Corner. http://www.carolinacorner.com/attractions/flood-forty-wataugas-worst-moment.htm (now inactive).

Documenting the American South (Wilson Library, University of North Carolina at Chapel Hill). https://docsouth unc.edu/.

Dunn Area Tourism Authority *Visitors Guide.* http://www.dunntourism .org/history-and-facts/.

Eastern Band of Cherokee Indians. https://ebci.com/.

Learn NC (UNC Chapel Hill School of Education). http://crdl.usg.edu/ collections/lnc/?Welcome.

National Oceanic and Atmospheric Administration. http://www.wpc .ncep.noaa.gov/tropical/rain/sehrcn1940.html.

Ncpedia (various). http://ncpedia.org

Tillery Farms. http://www.cct78.org/history-house.html.

Weather Underground. https://www.wunderground.com/hurricane/ archive/AL/1940.

WPAQG Voice of the Blue Ridge. http://www.wpaq740.com.